PORTRAITS
OF
AMERICAN
PRESIDENTS
Volume I
THE ROOSEVELT PRESIDENCY: FOUR INTIMATE PERSPECTIVES OF FDR

Edited by Kenneth W. Thompson

White Burkett Miller
Center of Public Affairs

Copyright © 1982 by

University Press of America, Inc.

P.O. Box 19101, Washington, D.C. 20036

Printed in the United States of America

ISBN (Perfect): 0-8191-2828-7
ISBN   (Cloth): 0-8191-2827-9

*Dedicated
To
The Memory
Of
Tommy The Cork
Tireless Interpreter of FDR*

TABLE OF CONTENTS

PREFACE

A pattern has emerged in the course of organizing Miller Center Forums which has led to the present volume. We have discovered that the leading authorities on particular presidents have helped the Center to draw others with common background to the University of Virginia. By "word of mouth advertising," they have encouraged their friends to come to Faulkner House. Their help has been of inestimable value to a fledgling public affairs center. It has enabled us to further presidential studies through the contributions of distinguished visitors to the understanding of contemporary presidents.

Partly by accident and partly by design, then, we have discovered our guests were turning the spotlight on certain American presidents. They were viewing an administration from different perspectives and vantage points. The product is a portrait, not a photograph; it helps us see the character and spirit of a leader, not the more or less important details a photograph tends to convey. It tells us what was central to his life and works, not what was peripheral. The photograph reveals what can be seen with the naked eye. The portrait shows one thing the photograph cannot reveal: the human essence of the person portrayed.

With this volume, we announce a new series of publications, *Portraits of American Presidents.* We are grateful to the University Press of America for making this series available to a wide audience. We hope the next volume will deal with the presidency of Lyndon Johnson and subsequent volumes with other presidents. In the Introduction, the editor traces the history of the Center's interest in the presidency of FDR.

INTRODUCTION

At some time or other, everyone has heard the phrase, "All roads lead to Rome (or Paris or Washington)." In the study of almost every aspect of the contemporary presidency, the Miller Center has found "all roads lead to FDR." The Commission on the Presidential Press Conference discovered that Roosevelt was the model. He appeared to thrive on the give and take of exchanges with reporters. He persuaded them to distinguish between answers for direct quotation and not for quotation, between background information and off-the-record information. He sought both formal and informal contacts with newspapermen. He met often with reporters.

On January 30, 1982, the country celebrated the centennial of Roosevelt's birth. In preparation of the event, the Miller Center invited during the course of the preceding year four of FDR's most intimate associates and family members to come to Charlottesville and discuss the Roosevelt presidency. Among the participants was Thomas G. (Tommy the Cork) Corcoran. He died later that year on December 6, 1981, one day before the anniversary of Pearl Harbor. One of Tommy's contemporaries, Kenneth Crawford, wrote his obituary in the *Washington Post* saying:

> Thomas Gardiner (Tommy) Corcoran, 80, a leading architect and lobbyist for much of the legislation establishing President Franklin D. Roosevelt's New Deal, who had been one of this city's most prominent lawyers since the early 1940s,

died of a pulmonary embolism yesterday in the Washington Hospital Center.

Mr. Corcoran and his colleague in government, Benjamin V. Cohen, were a team who came close to revolutionizing American government in the early New Deal days. In the process, Mr. Corcoran became an almost mythical hero to Rooseveltians, who viewed the New Deal as a bright light at the end of the tunnel of depression. By the same token, he became a symbol of irresponsibly destructive experimentation to Roosevelt's equally dedicated opponents.

He was not underrated in either camp. His legal scholarship, vitality and wit made him a formidable innovator and advocate. In the early 1930s, "Corcoran and Cohen" entered the language of political controversy as though the two names were a single word: "Corcorancone." It was a word much used in congressional campaign debate. In Wall Street and business board rooms it was a perjorative.

Yet when he left the government in 1940, Mr. Corcoran's law office was besieged by some of the same corporate leaders who most volubly had denounced him when he was a government official. So many became his clients that his law firm Corcoran, Foley, Youngman, and Rowe, grew and prospered through subsequent decades. Newspapers usually identified him in his private career as a lawyer-lobbyist. He called himself a lawyer-entrepeneur.

Mr. Corcoran and Cohen were among the first of the bright young Harvard Law School alumni recommended for service in the New Deal brain trust by Felix Frankfurter, than a professor on the school's faculty.

Both Mr. Corcoran and Cohen had practiced law in Wall Street and were knowledgeable about the operations of securities exchanges, so their first assignment was to draft the Securities Act of 1933. Under orders from the White House, but working with legislative leaders—especially House Speaker Sam Rayburn—they pushed the reform legislation through in record time.

Their collaboration later accounted for the Securities and Exchange Commission Act of 1935 and the Public Utilities Holding Company Act of 1935. They also contributed to the Federal Housing Administration Act of 1934.

Their reputations made by these successes, they went on to legislation establishing the Tennessee Valley Authority and Fair Labor Standards Board. They also took a hand in enactment of the Wage and Hour Law. These were among the most important and enduring of New Deal reforms.

The National Recovery Act, another key measure, which the Supreme Court ultimately invalidated, was not a Corcoran-

Cohen product. Neither was the so-called court-packing plan, which Congress rejected, although Mr. Corcoran supported it as an administration lobbyist.

Through all the years they worked together as a Roosevelt task force, contriving legislation that would stand up in the predominantly conservative courts and engineering it through congressional committees dominated by orthodox politicians, Mr. Corcoran and Cohen held relatively obscure positions in the executive bureaucracy. Neither ever was officially on the White House staff. Their salaries through most of their government careers were $8,000 a year.

Both bachelors, they lived with a group of congenial young lawyers in what was called "the little red house on R Street," the former summer residence of President U.S. Grant. In those times Mr. Corcoran and his friends were said to have a "passion for anonymity." Both felt that their jobs could be done out of the spotlight. By cooperating with certain reporters, they managed for a time to keep their names out of print or, at most, on the inside pages.

Whatever anonymity Mr. Corcoran and Cohen had achieved ended with the fight over the so-called "death sentence," imposed by the Utility Holding Company legislation.

Sen. Owen Brewster of Maine, who had been one of the supporters of the legislation, changed sides in mid-conflict. When Mr. Corcoran remonstrated with him, Brewster reported that he had been threatened with cancellation of plans for a hydroelectric plant in Maine.

At a congressional hearing, Mr. Corcoran denied threatening Brewster. Brewster called him a liar.

"We'll see who's a liar," Mr. Corcoran replied.

From then on, Mr. Corcoran's cover, such as it was, was blown. That committee, like many others over the years, failed to censure or even reprove Mr. Corcoran, who had a winning way with the House/Senate committees.

All pretense that the team of Corcoran and Cohen operated without White House credentials was abandoned after the Brewster uproar.

Mr. Corcoran did not have direct access to Roosevelt until 1935. Joseph P. Kennedy happened to remark to Roosevelt that Mr. Corcoran could sing admirable Irish ballads and sea chanties, and Mr. Corcoran was called to the White House, where he subsequently became a frequent guest and presidential counselor.

Mr. Corcoran became an invaluable administration operator, with a network of friends forged in the executive branch, federal agencies, and in Congress. He influenced judicial appointments and worked on the president's political speeches. He had a gift for the language that put lilt into oratory.

He traveled with the president on campaign trips and became involved in the unsuccessful attempt to "purge" certain anti-New Deal Democrats in the 1938 elections. Ten years later, Mr. Corcoran suffered another failure: the attempt to nominate William O. Douglas for president in place of Harry S. Truman.

Mr. Corcoran was born in Pawtucket, R.I. His father, Patrick, was the son of an Irish immigrant and a leading lawyer and Democratic politician. His mother's family had moved south from Nova Scotia.

At Brown University, Mr. Corcoran worked as a dance band pianist, won academic prizes, and was graduated at the head of his class. He moved on to Harvard Law School, where he again led his class, then became a law secretary to Justice Oliver Wendell Holmes, Jr. After an interlude at the court, Mr. Corcoran went to Wall Street, where he practiced from 1926 to 1932.

Mr. Corcoran came to Washington in 1932 to work for the Reconstruction Finance Corp. under Eugene Meyer. With the advent of the New Deal, the RFC became a model for several other government agencies and its personnel was scattered through them. Mr. Corcoran was transferred to the Treasury Department where he worked for Dean Acheson, then its under secretary. He later returned to the RFC, where he stayed for the remainder of his government career.

We dedicate this volume to Tommy the Cork who with Jim Rowe inaugurated our FDR series. None of us shall ever forget the sheer intellectual brilliance and unquenchable human vitality with which, at eighty, he approached the American presidency.

James H. Rowe, Jr. was Tommy the Cork's law partner and the first to inspire interest in an FDR colloquy at the Center. Secretary to Associate Justice Oliver Wendell Holmes and administrative assistant to President Roosevelt, Jim Rowe, by discussing other presidents with whom he worked before discussing Roosevelt, added a portrait of FDR seen in relation to his predecessor and successors. In serving, in effect, as an appointments secretary, Rowe witnessed Roosevelt's attitude toward his staff's relationship to the public and the press. He also conveyed FDR's activist view of government.

Franklin D. Roosevelt, Jr. was close to his father and a source of aid and comfort in difficult times. He went on to be a congressman and an under secretary of commerce under John F. Kennedy. His insights into his father's philosophy of government are both personal and illuminating, pointing up distinctions that most observers have overlooked.

Chalmers Roberts is one of America's most respected journalists. His career spans five decades and many newspapers but he began and ended with *The Washington Post*. Among reporters, Roberts has grown in stature because of his determination, as the British would say, "to get things right." This is reflected particularly in his concrete and revealing accounts of the form and substance of FDR's press conferences.

The four intimate portraits of President Roosevelt contained in this volume bespeak the unique insights of men who knew him well and observed him under fire. The portraits do not suffer from the admiration and affection of those who served him nor from their comparisons of him with others who held his high office. Other works, some more scholarly, will be published during the Roosevelt centennial but few if any will reflect the personal friendships that underlie the human and political vignette provided by these four uniquely positioned observers of FDR.

PRESIDENTS I HAVE KNOWN

James H. Rowe, Jr.

NARRATOR: We are pleased to welcome you to the Miller Center. The vital statistics on Jim Rowe's qualifications should be obvious. He's a graduate of the Harvard Law School and was secretary to Associate Justice of the Supreme Court, Oliver Wendell Holmes. From 1939 to 1941, he was administrative assistant to Mr. Roosevelt. He was a member of the staff of the Democratic National Committee, an assistant attorney general, and a member of the first Hoover Commission. He was also chairman of the Commission to Reorganize the Government of Puerto Rico in 1949, chairman of the Advisory Committee on Personnel to the Secretary of State, and was Counsel to the Senate Majority Policy Committee in 1946. He served as a naval officer in World War II and was decorated with two presidential citations, eight battle stars and a navy commendation ribbon. He's been the friend and confidant of five presidents.

From our standpoint not only has he met with Jim Young and myself informally on numerous occasions, but in addition he was a member of the Presidential Press Conference Commission that reviewed the organization of press conferences in the last six months. No one from this kind of background approaches the problems and the achievement of "The Presidents I Have Known," with greater authority and competency.

There is, in addition to the vital statistics, however, a human quality which comes through in all the memoirs and all the books. Just this morning I read a little account in the recent book on the Kennedys which referred to a consultation with Mr. Rowe regarding the reappointment to another post of Mr. Moyers, and the warmth and enthusiasm and vitality of his assessment of those who carry heavy burdens of office broke through in that evaluation.

1

We've been pleased whenever he's graced these tables to benefit from the verve and the flair and the enthusiasm that he brings to every subject he addressed. It's a great honor for us to welcome Mr. James Rowe.

MR. ROWE: Thank, you, Ken. This is going to be an egocentric and arrogant talk and the reason for it is that Ken called and said, "Would you come down and talk about presidential leadership?" I said, "You know, I don't think anybody understands what presidential leadership is, and maybe I can talk about presidents I have known." So he said, "All right," and this is what you're going to hear. You'll find a lot of "I"'s in this and ego, but I will try to keep it down and I will try to be brief enough to try to talk about twenty minutes and then maybe you can ask questions about presidents you're interested in.

I should say something about presidential leadership. I don't know how to define it or describe it, but I do know it when I see it. I know, for instance, Franklin Roosevelt had presidential leadership. There was never any question about it. I know that Hoover and Carter did not, maybe because they were engineers. They didn't have it. Roosevelt had it all the time. I think what we should look for, or what I look for, in a president or a candidate for president is intelligence. He should, I think, be a professional politician, spend his life in it. I'm convinced of that. Maybe after our last president, I think he should have a flair for what's going on in the world. I think he should not be ideological; the best ones weren't. And that, I think, is almost all I can say about presidential leadership until we get to the questions.

Mr. Reagan is not on my list to talk about. He is, I suppose, a professional politician. He's been campaigning for a long time. He was governor of our largest state, as was Franklin Roosevelt, at the time, governor of our largest state. The thing we probably ignore about Roosevelt is he spent eight years in Washington as assistant secretary in the Navy, including the war years, and if you looked at his appointments the young New Dealers were young, but the older men had all been young men of the Wilson camp. Joe Davies, oh, I could name ten or twenty. Louis Brownlow was commissioner of the District of Columbia in World War I.

I'm not going to talk about the presidents I have known chronologically but sort of peripherally, because I knew them in many different ways. I knew FDR very well because I spent four years in the White House as an administrative assistant. I finally went to him and told him I really thought it was a great job, but it seemed to be qualifying me only to be president, and I didn't think I would be, so could I go over to the Department of Justice, and he sent me over there. The other good friend I had was Lyndon Johnson because I got to the White House just as he got to Congress, and we were friends in our youth and friends ever since, all the way through until he died. The others I'm going to mention are Harry Truman, Jack Kennedy, and Herbert Hoover.

I didn't know Hoover when he was president. I was a college student then, but years after I was on the first Hoover Commission. Speaker Rayburn appointed me to that. Hoover was the chairman and I got to know him, I think, quite well. We disagreed, I may say, about everything. I was a flamboyant convinced New Dealer and he thought the world would be better off without the New Deal, and this is what we struggled with during the commission. In fact, it was as clear to him as it was to me—the commission started in 1947—that Mr. Truman would be out of office in 1948. Tom Dewey would come in and, really, we were going to abolish the whole New Deal. That's the way he went at it and I was kicking and screaming all the way. I may say, Dean Acheson who was on the commission was a little more polite than I was. But all this ended when Mr. Truman was reelected, to Mr. Hoover's great surprise and to my great surprise, and so we backed off and we really did a reorganization job. A lot of good work was done. The Health, Education and Welfare predecessor was done by Hoover. He created the GSA, something that's not been so successful since, but he was the originator of it, with Truman's help and the Congress's help.

Just to get some kind of perspective about life, Hoover's last budget when he was president was four billion dollars, Roosevelt's last peace time budget was nine billion, and Johnson, when he had his first budget, he kicked and screamed to make sure it stayed under a hundred billion dollars. Now it's seven hundred billion. I don't know where we're going from here. Mr. Reagan, I think, is going to cut it some, I hope.

Mr. Hoover was an austere man. I remember he would summon me fairly often to have breakfast with him at the Mayflower where he stayed when he was in Washington—he lived in New York. I would get there about seven-thirty and we would have bacon and eggs. I remember waiting until about ten-thirty and we sort of sat and looked at each other and I kept puzzling, why has he got me here, what is he going to convince me of. He never convinced me of anything. But I think he was merely being kind and friendly, social to his opponents. He was a tremendous worker—I'm still talking about the commission and I assume he was also as president. We would have meetings all week and he would get on a train to go to New York Saturday afternoon, and he would tell us, "Be back here at nine o'clock on Monday and I will have some reports." He would go up and work all the way on the train, all the time in New York, and come back in the train and put on our desk three written reports on Monday morning. I don't know how he could do it, physically, but he did do it. He and Truman were great friends, I think, because Roosevelt never let him in the White House. Roosevelt always campaigned against him. As soon as the commission was set up Truman would have him over for lunch or dinner or something of that kind, and they became great friends.

Then in the campaign of 1948, Truman got on his whistle-stop train and he went out campaigning against Hoover. And Mr. Hoover got his feelings hurt, surprisingly. We were sitting in a room together, just the two of us, and he said to me, "Now, how could President Truman do this?" and I said, "Mr. President, you've been in politics; he's running for reelection; you shouldn't take it seriously." But, he did take it seriously, he was quite crushed. After the election I sent word to the White House that President Truman had hurt President Hoover's feelings. Truman got him right over, patted him on the shoulder and said, "None of that was personal, you know that." So they were again quite good friends.

I now turn to Roosevelt. Someone once said that every man has his heroes before he's thirty. Well, I was in the White House when I was twenty-eight, and he's still my hero. He is still the standard to which we should all repair, in my view, as president. He was all charm. You've all heard about the charm, and if you met him you know about the charm. His staff adored him. In the back room when we were working, his charm would sort of disappear.

He was all business. It's hard to tell stories because I have so many about Roosevelt. I do remember two which I will tell you quickly—I told you there's going to be a lot of ego and "I" in this. He used to say, "You're a bird dog and I'm going to send you out to do various jobs." He sent me out once, I can't remember what the job was, but I came back and reported: "This is what it is, Mr. President." And he had a habit of looking up at the ceiling and he said,"You know, there was some fellow in here the other day. I can't remember who he was, but he told me such and such. Did you run into that?" Then I realized I hadn't turned all those stones over, I missed. After you got caught that way a couple of times you would do your homework very carefully.

The other story I remember, we wanted to move Leon Henderson from one place to another, and he said, "I want to do this but you go out and talk to some people and tell me how it should be done." So I came back: "Leon should be moved, Mr. President, and this is the way it should be done." "Well," he said, "I think you're right, I have to move him, but I'm going to do it this way." Well, I think I'd reached twenty-nine at this point so I said, "Mr. President, I don't think you should do it that way, I think you should do it the way I suggested it. It saves you a lot of trouble." And he said, "Well, no, I think I'll do it the way I suggested." And still, since I was twenty-nine, I came back the third time and said, "Now, Mr. President, if you don't do it my way I think you're going to have a little trouble.'' He smiled and said, ''Jim, we're going to do it my way and I'll tell you why.'' He said, ''The American people may have made a mistake but they elected me president, not you!'' And I said, ''Yes Sir!'' In other words, when he made up his mind, that was it. You shouldn't fool around any longer.

He didn't like public controversy, but I think he used it as a tool. He liked to have Harry Ickes and Harry Hopkins out there fighting in public, or Jesse Jones and Henry Wallace, because he could make a pretty good judgment on the reaction of the people or the newspapers or the politicians. So he encouraged it. He just let everybody fight longer than we would have thought he should.

His other quality, I think, as a politician was he never tried to get too far ahead of the American people in his judgment. In 1937 he went to Chicago and made the quarantine speech about perhaps using the Navy to quarantine the Nazis' and the fascists' shipping and the reaction was so strong against it he really just pulled back for a while. He was always trying to help the allies but he didn't know how far he could go. I can remember, I think it was late 1941, I went in to talk to him about some minor point and he looked rather crestfallen. He said, ''The Japanese are moving their troops south; they're moving them into Indonesia, maybe Singapore, certainly more into Manchuria, and there's nothing I can do about it. The American people will not let me use the Navy to stop them.'' He looked very discouraged. Of course Pearl Harbor came along and solved most of that kind of problem, but he was always watching the American people, how far he could go, what the Congress was doing. He once said—and I think this is why he did it—he said someone wanted to be Solicitor General and Roosevelt owed him a lot and he should have made him Solicitor General, but he said, ''You know, we're getting into trouble in the world. I've got to deal with the Senate and the Senate has to confirm, and I was here in the Wilson days and remember all the trouble Wilson had. I'm not going to get crossed up with the Senate.'' These are the touchstones. He was essentially a politician, practically all the time. I use that in the good sense. A lot of people use it in a different sense.

I now come to Mr. Truman. I was in the Navy and I came back once and went in to see FDR after the election and after he picked Truman. I was rather puzzled about why he picked Truman. I thought he was going to pick Sam Rayburn. I said, ''Mr. President, why did you pick Truman?'' He was a minor senator. He'd done a good job on the investigations committee during the war but nothing else. He came out of what—you have to call it frankly—was a corrupt political machine. New Dealers were always snobbish about Truman. He was regarded as a bankrupt haberdasher who came out of that machine, never went to college. When he was president he had cronies around him who took fur coats and refrigerators and we had not too high an opinion of him. So I was puzzled. Well, he told me an interesting story. He said, "Here I was running in 1944 and none of the candidates for vice president could help me. I wanted to pick the one who'd hurt me least. Henry Wallace had been vice president, the bosses just marched in and said, 'You can't have him, we won't take him.' Senator Bankhead of Alabama was a candidate and the liberals of the labor movement won't take him.''

Jimmy Byrnes really wanted to be vice president and Roosevelt explored that. Jimmy Byrnes had begun life as a Catholic. I think his mother—I'm not sure of my facts—remarried and he was brought up an Episcopalian, but Roosevelt was not too sure how the Catholic vote would take this. He sent an emissary to the Cardinals, one in Chicago and one in New York and said, "How would this effect Jimmy Byrnes, and me?" And the Cardinals said, "Well since he was a little boy who changed, it wouldn't be any problem." But then he asked the labor movement and they said, "Oh no, we won't take Byrnes." So he said, "I picked Truman because labor liked him, the bosses liked him, and the southerners liked him. I concluded he was the one who would hurt me least." In all our conversation there was no discussion about whether he might be a good president, and of course a few months later Roosevelt was dead. Retroactively, he was a very good choice it seems. He was a superb president for foreign policy: Korea, the Marshall Plan, Turkey and Greece; and he always had the good instinct for the right thing to do. He made decisions quite easily. So all in all, he probably was a pretty good president, a considerably good president.

He was a very human man. I heard a story just the other day I'd never heard of. There was a man named McDonald who was a Securities and Exchange Commissioner. He was a Republican. You always had to have three Democrats and two Republicans. One day Truman made him chairman of this commission. This was the pride and joy of the New Deal, the Securities and Exchange Commission, and everybody wondered why he picked this Republican. Well, it turned out that McDonald was a bachelor and he wandered around Lafayette Square on Saturday nights, just liked to wander around the White House, and at that time Truman was living in Blair House across the street. So McDonald said to himself one night, "I think I'll go visit the president." So he walked up the steps of Blair House, rang the bell, and said, "I'd like to see President Truman." And they said, "Who are you?" And he said, "I'm SEC Commissioner McDonald." And in a minute he was invited in. Truman said, "Come in," and they each sat down. They had a bourbon and were talking. McDonald said, "Mr. President, I see you have your piano over in that corner and I know you play the piano. Well, I'm quite a singer." He said, "If you'll play I'll sing." Truman said, "All right," and they spent the rest of the night drinking bourbon and singing and playing. Every month or so McDonald would wander up, press the doorbell, and say, "Is the president in?" Truman would play the piano and McDonald would sing. I guess he was a pretty good singer, Truman kept letting him in.

As soon as he became president he fired Francis Biddle who was the attorney general under Roosevelt, and out he went with a sort of clatter. Biddle was sort of a classic fellow himself and after, I think, six months he said to his wife, "I think I'll invite President Truman to dinner," and Katherine said, "He won't come." Francis said, "Let's find out." He went to the phone, called Truman, Truman got on the phone and he said, "Mr. President, I'd like to have you to dinner." "Fine," said Truman, and he came on out. Truman later made him America's judge at the Nuremburg trials.

And now we get down to Jack Kennedy. I used to say that Roosevelt was a man of style and substance, Kennedy had style and Lyndon Johnson had substance. I really knew Jack Kennedy best in the 1960 campaign. I was first supporting Hubert Humphrey and then Lyndon Johnson. I was always against Kennedy. But as I watched him around the country—I was out battling for delegates and Kennedy was out trying to get his own delegates—I found him, I think, the best national politician since Roosevelt. He understood where the strength was in each state far better than Johnson or Humphrey or, I think, anybody that I had run into except Roosevelt.

I think there are two reasons for that. The first is rather mundane. He ran for the vice presidential nomination in 1956. Adlai Stevenson threw the convention open in 1956 and Kennedy made a great run for it on television. Because of that, after the convention, all the politicians wanted him to come and speak in their states and he got around the country speaking at their dinners. That way he learned a great deal about the United States, far more than Johnson and Humphrey or anybody. The other reason: I think he was about the most detached man I've ever run into. We'd get out somewhere and Kennedy would see me moving around and say, "Where have you been, Jim?" I would tell him what state, let's say Oregon, and then he'd say, "Well, how do I look?" "Well," I said, "you've got strength here, you've got strength over there. Hubert or Lyndon—whichever one it was—is ahead of you there." And he would say, "Well, I think you're right about that, and you're right about that but I'm not so sure about over there." He was as hard boiled talking about himself as I was talking about him. I thought it was a remarkable quality.

In the convention, of course, he ran over Johnson, whom I was supporting at that time. Then he picked Lyndon Johnson for vice president. I don't think he wanted him, but I think he knew he needed him for Texas and the South. He just felt he didn't have enough electoral votes unless he got Johnson to pull him through.

All of Kennedy's staff were against Johnson, labor and liberals were against Johnson, and everybody was except Jack Kennedy. He picked him and he won.

I think he might have been a great president if he had lived. Maybe he was too detached. Kennedy would ask some certain senators to vote for a bill of his and if a senator didn't want to, he'd say, "I'd love to, but it would just murder me in my state. I just can't do it." And Kennedy would say, "Well, ok." Now Lyndon Johnson would call that same fellow up and he knew what he was going to say. But before he could get his mouth open Johnson had him by the lapels, waving the American flag and saying, "You've got to be a patriot," and shove him out the door with a commitment. That was the difference between the two of them.

I think Lyndon Johnson, of at least five presidents I've talked about, I think Lyndon Johnson was the brightest. He was just as bright as anybody you've ever seen. He was certainly the most complicated man, and I think he was the most insecure man. I don't know why he was insecure. I'm not a psychiatrist but it always kept cropping up. He did more for education and civil rights than any other president. Education, I think because he used to teach these young Mexicans and he saw how little they had. This is really why we've been pouring so much money into education, because Johnson did it. I don't know if we're going to get results for it. Civil rights, I don't think these bills would have passed. I think only a southerner could have done it. I used to tell him that. I said, "You've got to run for president because I don't see any solution for this country unless you do it." A southerner had to do it and he did it. I don't know where the end of that road is yet but Johnson is the fellow who started it. I think he was the best parliamentarian. He's certainly the greatest Senate Majority Leader we've ever had. I think as a parliamentarian maybe Winston Churchill was better, but Churchill had an easier job.

Vietnam did bring him down. He finally cut his losses when the Army wanted 206,000 more troops. Purely by luck I happened to see him that day. Dean Acheson, and Mac Bundy, and all the wise men, the generals, the older men whom he talked to, they switched on him that day. They'd always been for Vietnam, then they turned against it. I was going in to see him with Teddy White who writes the biographies of the "Making of the President." Johnson never would see Teddy because Teddy had written some mean things about him. Finally, he said to me he'd see Teddy, a friend of mine. He said, "I'll do that for you." He always was "doing" something for somebody else so he could get a favor out of it later. Teddy and I sat around and waited for hours. We finally got in and Johnson was just exhausted. He sort of grumbled at Ted, he didn't like him, and finally I said, "Look, Mr. President, this fellow is trying to write some history and maybe you ought to talk to him." Johnson started and what he talked about was very interesting. He started comparing himself with Roosevelt, all the things that Roosevelt had done and what he had done. He said, "Maybe I've done as much as Roosevelt." He was exhausted and tired and it really sounded like a valedictory speech about how many things he had accomplished. Then we left and I said, "Now Teddy, don't pay attention to that tone. He's always up and he's always down and don't pay any attention to the valedictory." One week later he quit.

I don't know Carter so I can't tell you about Carter and Rowe. I can tell you one story, which I shouldn't. Mrs. Rowe and I were invited on January 15, to the White House to a reception and I said, "Well, you know, this is pretty clear. I'm going as an 'accompanying spouse' because Mrs. Rowe is on the White House Historical Association." That's the outfit that sells you the pamphlets when you go on tour of the White House and they take the money and buy paintings and furniture. I said, "So there I am, I'm an 'accompanying spouse.'" I was saying this to Tim Stanley who was a friend of mine, "You know, Tim, this is a little demeaning after having spent four years with Roosevelt and end up as an 'accompanying spouse.'" Tim said, "Well, that is demeaning, but think of me. I was in the White House with Eisenhower and whenever I go now I go as the father of Christopher who's a playmate of Amy." And sure enough that's what it was.

There were about a hundred fifty people there and they were all—if I may use the phrase—"fat cats" who had given the White House something nice, then this historical association crowd, and a lot of what seemed to me rather rough-hewn people. I decided these fellows must be Houston oil men. President Carter and Mrs. Carter talked about the White House, both very moving I might add, very touching. They were saying who was there and my rough-hewn oil men turned out to be the carpenters, plumbers, and the gardeners at the White House. He praised them very highly and then said, "I can't shake hands with you, I'm just getting my harness off, but if you want to go through the White House, you've done a lot for it, go ahead. Don't come into our private quarters because all our boxes are being packed. They have to be out by today."

So, we wandered through the first floor and looked at it. It's a beautiful house. Then we decided to go up to the second floor, Lincoln's bedroom, Queen Elizabeth's bedroom, I forgot who else's. And I said to Mrs. Rowe, "Let's go up and look," and she said, "let's take the elevator." So we went over and got in the elevator. As we were going up she got chatting to the elevator operator and told him, "The first time I was ever in this elevator I was with Franklin Roosevelt and my skirt fell off." He sort of looked at her. She said, "I had on my sister's new dress and she was bigger than I was." We were all laughing and we got to the top and opened it and there was Jimmy Carter looking at us and we looking at him. He

9

was in his jogging clothes. I said, "Mr. President—" My wife who is faster than I am said, "Fine speech last night, Mr. President." He said, "Thank you," and disappeared into the dark. I don't know if I'll ever see him again or not.

That's a good place to stop.

NARRATOR: We're very glad, at least for the University of Virginia, Mr. Rowe has not disappeared in the dark. One story he didn't tell which I think several of us would hope he might repeat concerns the change that has apparently taken place in the public role of advisers and assistants to presidents. In his day it wasn't common for presidential advisers to have press offices and public relations assistants. It wasn't common, or at least it wasn't encouraged, to appear in places where they would get the amount of public attention that some of our public figures have had in recent years. Would you be willing to tell us President Roosevelt's attitude about the public activities of his assistants?

MR. ROWE: Unfriendly! I remember, we were appointed as assistants who had a passion for anonymity and that's really what he expected. I can remember once I went in to see him and he said, "Didn't I read in the *Star*, in some social column, that you were at some cocktail party yesterday?" I said, "Yes, Mr. President." He said, "If I read that too often you're going to need another job." He made it perfectly clear that there was only one man running for office around there. We did stay away from the newspapermen. Steve Early was the press secretary, and a good one, and he was the man to deal with the press. The rest of us were not out leaking this or leaking that. We really would have got bounced, I think. I didn't press him on that point.

QUESTION: I was just wondering if you might like to expand on that question, your view of the role of the presidential staff. It's a huge staff now. What are your thoughts about its current position?

MR. ROWE: I still think the Roosevelt view is correct. We were just a handful. He had three secretaries and six administrative assistants until the war. Then, the White House staff started building up, a little ahead of the war. Jimmy Byrnes left the Supreme Court and Judge Vinson left the Court of Appeals Bench to work at the White House. Until then, we were a very small group. Of course, Washington was small and we also knew everybody in Washington. We knew the senators, we knew the congressmen, we knew the people in the executive branch. We did not think our function was to explain to the press what we were doing. That was for cabinet members.

Another time I got in trouble was when some cabinet member

went to the president and complained that I was keeping him away from the president. It wasn't true but the president called me on the carpet. I said, "This just doesn't happen to be true, Mr. President." "Well," he said, "if cabinet members get the impression that you're blocking them from me you're going to need another job." It was one of his favorite phrases. I sometimes wonder how I made it. But he felt that way: "The Cabinet should get in when they want to see me." Some of them were bores and he sort of wouldn't let them in on his own, but he didn't want his staff getting in between him and the Cabinet.

When I came back after the war and President Truman was in office, I asked a couple of my friends who were working for him, "Who does this in the White House that I used to do, and who does what I did?" And I finally said, "You've got nine people doing what I did!" It's just grown, and grown, and grown. Every president has gone in there announcing he's going to cut down. Lyndon Johnson was thumping tables that he was going to cut down. He ended up—each president ends up—with more than the other. I do not know why. Therefore, they're all over town, they're leaking everything. Some things they should, I suppose, and some they shouldn't. I personally think it's a bad practice. But again, it's one of these things I don't know what can be done about it.

Looking at Reagan, Dick Scammon is a great political expert. He ran the Census Bureau, and he's an expert on polling. He does it for CBS. I ran into him the other day. He was saying that in his lifetime he thought he had seen three good communicators, one was Roosevelt, one was Kennedy and maybe now Reagan. Maybe Reagan is going to do a great deal of this himself. He lets Meese speak and that's about all, in the White House. I don't think he can let everybody run around telling cabinet officers what to do and telling the press. It's a long answer and I hope it answers your question.

QUESTION: Could you say something about the relationship between presidential leadership and popularity? It's a rather difficult question, I know, but as I've listened to you you've talked about presidential leadership in terms of, say, Roosevelt exercising leadership by having a very fine sense of where the country is and where it's prepared to go. Obviously, that's an admirable characteristic for a president to have. But there's another aspect of leadership and that is sensing that the people really ought to be going some place where they don't yet want to go. Do you have any sense of how those two things interact, and whether the second option is really a terribly viable one?

MR. ROWE: I think the best example, I suppose, is Roosevelt trying to push the country toward helping the allies. He made very hard-boiled political judgments about how far he could take the country. He obviously thought we should be helping England long before we did. The country was not ready, particularly the West and Middle West, I suppose, where the isolationist strength was then. I think this was his judgment: how far can I push and how fast? He made an early mistake pushing too fast. A lot of people felt because of that he made a mistake of not pushing harder later. I think it's a very tough political judgment of how far you can take it. If you get too far ahead, you're gone. I think Jimmy Carter often got too far ahead and people didn't know what he was talking about, really. I don't think he had any sense of that. I think Roosevelt did. I think, curiously, Truman had a lot of that. You could say maybe Eisenhower had, but I can't define it.

QUESTION: You mentioned ways in which Roosevelt had a sense of what the people would accept, or perhaps when he had gone a little further than what they would accept. In the latter part of Nixon's administration it was quite clear that he became quite out of touch with what was going on. What are some of the ways in which a president learns over a period of time what the people will accept or not?

MR. ROWE: Well, I'm not sure. You know, speaking of presidents making mistakes, the three great landslides in this country were Roosevelt in 1936, Johnson in 1964 and Nixon in 1972, and because of those landslides, at least in my view, all three of them were in trouble within two or three months. Roosevelt and the court packing plan, Johnson and Vietnam, Nixon and Watergate. I think maybe if they do so well they get a little arrogant.

There's another thing that I think happens with presidents and I think it happened with Roosevelt. It's a very natural thing. A president never really sees anybody unless that somebody wants something from the president, whether it's a senator, congressman, Cabinet officer, businessman, labor leader. It's a wearing business. Therefore, I think they have the tendency, the longer they're in office, to retreat and spend their time with their staff. Roosevelt did that, I think Truman did that, and Nixon, all of them did. With Carter I think Camp David helped some. I think they get out of touch the longer they're in office. But I don't know of any way of getting out of it. I suppose if they have old friends who were senators and congressman who would try to tell them, maybe it would work. Usually it doesn't, in my view.

QUESTION: Can you comment on the role of presidential wives, the ones that you know?

MR. ROWE: Let me see, I don't know any of them too well. Mrs. Roosevelt, she was a great politician, she was a professional politician. I'll say this, she tried to get me fired twice—she didn't try to get me fired, but the bosses did, Jim Farley, Ed Flynn, both Democratic National Chairmen. I used to handle appointments and we used to quarrel quite often about it. I used to think I was in favor of competent appointments and they wanted—as Governor Dave Lawrence put it one day: I was talking about Grace Kelly's father who was county chairman of Philadelphia, and I said, "How is he? He's a great speaker but how good is he?" Dave said, "Well, he always likes to be on the platform making speeches, Jim, but the day after the election when we had won and when he ought to be in pounding the table to get some poor slob who doesn't deserve it a good job, Jack is never there." They wanted jobs for the slobs! I used to have fights.

It was very interesting to me. Farley did not go to Roosevelt to complain about me, and Ed Flynn, who was later Democratic chairman, didn't go to Roosevelt. They went to Mrs. Roosevelt and said to her, "Well, you go to the president and tell him what a troublesome fellow Jim Rowe is." The reason for that is that she came from New York and they had earlier brought her into New York politics. She came up through the regular organization and these were the people she respected and she would do it for them. She did. Fortunately, he didn't fire me either. I keep indicating as I talk that I had a perilous life, but I don't really think so.

QUESTION: How would you compare her role to Rosalynn Carter's?

MR. ROWE: Well, first of all the president didn't get out and she did get out and she was in that sense his eyes and ears. She got to all sorts of places. I don't know, maybe Mrs. Carter was a strong—some people say a strong president. Mrs. Roosevelt stayed in the role of wife, but she did a lot of reporting. We used to get mad at her because she used to come in during the president's cocktail hour and start to report then. We didn't like that very much, when he should be relaxing. But, she was a powerful woman and she was a powerful woman in the government. She was into all parts of the government, the things that interested her. I can't say much about any other presidential wife, but she always knew what was going on. She was the great, not the great, well maybe, she was the great liberal influence on Roosevelt.

QUESTION: Mr. Rowe, you referred a few minutes ago to FDR's relations to people on Capitol Hill, coming to him because they wanted something. This is a subject that interests me. Would you elaborate upon that? How frequently did he see people when Congress was in session? Which senators, congressmen did he like, dislike, etc.?

MR. ROWE: He liked Jimmy Byrnes because Jimmy Byrnes was a great senator, I think; not so good as a governor or maybe a judge or maybe a secretary of state, but he was a superb senator. My feeling about Jimmy is, he was always giving advice, he was not after this or after that. He wanted to be president. Byrnes was a great favorite. Young Bob La Follette was a great friend of his. Claude Pepper was a great friend because he was sort of Roosevelt's spear. Some conservative senator would go after Roosevelt on the Senate floor and the next day Claude would be in there with, not precisely a meat cleaver, but sort of a scalpel.

He saw a great number of senators and congressmen. I'm interested in watching this because I think he saw many more than any president I know, both on the record and off the record. He always—and I think all presidents do—had a large number of visitors through the back door that nobody knows anything about. I think any congressman could get in pretty quickly to see Roosevelt.

QUESTION: Senator Wagner, he was a very close friend?

MR. ROWE: Wagner, yes, because Wagner had done so much legislation. If you look at the Roosevelt legislation you can almost say most of it was Wagner's. He saw them, knew them, I think far more than is done today, because I think Washington is more complicated.

You've probably heard the story of Lyndon Johnson going to see him, I'm sure most people have, with the request for a dam down there in his district. You didn't get much from a Roosevelt appointment because he would "filibuster" you. I remember he did it to me when I was trying to get appointments through. We'd sit down and have lunch and he told me all about Hyde Park. I once knew more about Hyde Park than any living person! Well, young Congressman Johnson came in and he was told by Watson, the appointment secretary, he'd have fifteen minutes. But Roosevelt started talking and Johnson didn't get a word in. Out the door he went and he complained bitterly to the staff. It took us all of two weeks to get him back in. This time Johnson came in the door talking at top speed. He did get his dam.

You know, Roosevelt knew a great deal of what was going on, and I don't know where he got it. Johnson was a telephone president, he was never off the thing. I don't think Roosevelt was on the phone that much but he talked to an awful lot of people and knew a great deal of what was going on.

QUESTION: Would you expand on your comment about the comparative lack of substance in Kennedy?

MR. ROWE: Well, that is an unfair comment because he might have got a lot of that legislation through if he lived another year or so. He made great speeches. I don't think he worked as hard at the job as maybe I thought he should. Again, I think that quality of detachment I talked about sort of bothers me. He didn't twist their arms and hit them over the head the way Johnson or Roosevelt did when they wanted something. He'd been a playboy congressman, an indifferent senator, great campaigner. I just don't know. I may be unfair. It's not a matter of prejudice. I liked Jack Kennedy a great deal. But he didn't work at it the way I was talking about, like Johnson seeing people all the time. It was this quality of detachment.

QUESTION: Mr. Rowe, the power of the presidency, as I've watched it across the spectrum, has been eroded. The staffs of the White House, the Congress, the swollen bureaucracy, it's almost like they're running the government and not elected or appointed officials. Could you address that as you've seen it progress over the years?

MR. ROWE: I think there is a lot of truth in that. I am really startled when we talk about the Congress. There are thirty thousand people up there on the staff. I remember when I was in the government, if I had a problem I'd go down and see Senator X and we'd discuss it and he'd say: "I will," or "I won't," or "I'll look into this and come back in a day or so." And I'd come back in a few days and see the senator. Today if you go down and see Senator X he'll say, "Well, yes, I know what you're talking about, but talk to my staff." You never do get back in to see the senator. They have become administrators. They've just got too much staff which fall all over each other.

This is certainly more true of the executive branch, and I think it's true of the White House. I've been preaching, with a notable complete lack of success, since I left the White House to cut down the White House staff. Nobody's done it yet and I don't think they ever will. But, they don't need all those people.

Speaking generally of the government, when I've been in it or when I've dealt with it from the outside, in the old days you used to start with two or three people and if you talked to those two or three people and they agreed you could move. Today, you have to talk to about twenty-three, and by the time you get to the twenty-third the first three have died, or left office, and you have to start all over again. I'm surprised anything happens in government.

QUESTION: How do you assess Eisenhower today?

MR. ROWE: Well, I thought he was—as we all did—a great general, a nice quiet president; didn't bother us. The country wanted someone like that. As you may or may not know, there's a new theory. There's a professor at Princeton that's got his nose in all those papers up there and Eisenhower comes out quite differently. He may have given the country the impression he was playing golf, and he was doing this, and he was doing that, but his papers indicate that he was sort of behind the scenes in instructing his staff. He was telling Sherman Adams, "Go do that, get that done over there, and you go out front." They tell the story—you may have heard of Jim Hagerty as one of the great press secretaries. Eisenhower said one day, "Jim, you go out and tell the press such and such." And Haggerty said, "Mr. President, if I do that they'll lynch me." Eisenhower got up out of his chair and came around and put his arm around him and said, "Better you than me, Jim." I think there was a lot of that.

QUESTION: Could you talk a little bit about the influence of Keynesian economics on Roosevelt, and then on Johnson in the period of the late sixties when there were warnings about inflation and so on? To what extent were you worried about that?

MR. ROWE: Well we were all Keynesians, the New Dealers, including Roosevelt. Roosevelt saw Keynes several times. I never really understood Keynes. I don't know if we knew what we were supposed to think. But, I think we followed the doctrine pretty much in those days.

I don't think any president really understood economics. In fact, I'm not sure the economists understood it, looking at their record. But there have always been a number around. I think they try, but I don't think presidents are really capable of following theory very much. I think they get a feel for it. A good president gets a feel to go to this way or that way. Maybe Reagan can do that pretty well, I don't know. Still, the economists, as you know, have not been a great success.

QUESTION: I don't mean to suggest that the situation that has been inherited by Mr. Reagan is an exact parallel to the economic difficulties that were inherited by President Roosevelt. But there are certain similarities, I think, to those of us who lived then and who have continued to live until now. We can recognize certain old enemies as well as old friends. I wonder if you would care to comment on the difference between what Mr. Roosevelt said to the American people in his famous remark, "We have nothing to fear but fear itself," and what Reagan has said about the economy falling apart and what a low point we've gotten to; scaring us in other words. Is that a significant difference?

MR. ROWE: I'm not sure. I've watched Mr. Reagan, but I don't know where Mr. Reagan is going to end up. As a violent partisan Democrat I do not think I'm the best witness you can find on the subject! I do think, in my better moments, Reagan got elected wearing Roosevelt's hat. I see remarkable things. He got forty-four percent of the labor vote. He went after that hammer and tong. He kept telling them he was a union leader. He was always quoting Roosevelt.

The first time I saw Reagan—I'd like to point this out—was in 1952 when Adlai Stevenson was running and I was his advance man in Los Angeles and Hollywood. I noticed on the platform—because he was pointed out—Ronald Reagan. He was head of the union, he was a famous actor, and if you wanted crowds in Los Angeles in those days, you got actors and actresses. And there was Ronald Reagan on the Democratic platform.

I think there's a parallel in a sense between Roosevelt and Reagan in the way they go after things. I think it's probably a conscious parallel with Reagan. I think he is scaring us but I think maybe we need to be scared. And I think he's going to get a great deal of what he's asking for. Now, whether that works I don't know. It's a rather happy position for partisans like me because if he does all this, we're all better off, and if he doesn't do it, we Democrats can scream.

QUESTION: What you were just saying reminds me of a question I've been brooding about. Ronald Reagan seems to be some kind of odd, new blend of Franklin Roosevelt and Harry Byrd. I was thinking, when you were with President Roosevelt, there was this famous little fight between Harry Byrd, Sr., on one side and Mr. Roosevelt on the other over a judgeship. Mr. Roosevelt lost. He underestimated his opposition in the Senate. What happened and what did Roosevelt really think of Harry Byrd?

MR. ROWE: He didn't like him! I do remember that. At that period there was a so-called liberal Virginia governor, Price, I think was his name. And we decided, in our wisdom, that we were going to build a new, good liberal party down here. I was put in charge of making sure all the patronage went to Price. I worked at it for about three months until Roosevelt wanted something and Byrd had it, you know.

On the judgeship, we didn't think we were going to win but we didn't think we were going to get shellacked. Roosevelt got three votes and Byrd got all the rest of them. So I do not think, until Carter, any president had tried again to go against the senator of the particular state. You know, that's a plum up there and they all said, "Well if he does it to Byrd he'll do it to us next month." So they all stuck together. I do remember that fight very well. I think a president can occasionally beat a senator if it's an appeals court appointment. This is to more than one state. But if it's a district judge, you can't beat the senator.

QUESTION: Maybe somebody should tell Mr. Rowe about what Armistead Dobie, then Dean of Virginia Law School, later District Court Judge of the Fourth Circuit, appointed by Roosevelt, replied when somebody asked him why he supported Mr. Roosevelt. He said, "Because he gave me a job, and then he gave me a better job!"

MR. ROWE: That was like the famous statement of my professor of constitutional law at Harvard, Thomas Reed Powell. Massachusetts passed a teacher's oath. In other words, you couldn't teach unless you took the oath. Harvard was in a great furor: "We won't sign this, we won't sign that. And someone asked Reed Powell, "Are you going to sign an oath supporting the Constitution?" He said, "Heavens yes, it has supported me for years."

QUESTION: My question is really in relation to the fifty destroyer deal with England. That was handled so astutely by President Roosevelt, to get across to the nation that we were not giving these ships. It might have been contrary to law to give them so we'll have a deal. The American people like a deal. How astute that was, the way he got these fellows on his yacht to talk to them.

It's customary to say that FDR was his own secretary of state, but was there somebody that you could identify in your days in the White House that you could say had more influence than any others on FDR's foreign policy posture, and his way of handling the American public? That was an extreme example of a very, very shrewd way of getting across something that could have exploded in his face.

MR. ROWE: Well, I think for that particular thing he had a good lawyer. He didn't have the attorney general. He didn't have the legal adviser in the State Department. They were sort of against it. He got Ben Cohen and Ben is the best lawyer that I know. He's eighty-six now, he's still the best lawyer. Ben did the drafting of all that.

QUESTION: Bob Jackson wrote an opinion as attorney general supporting that.

MR. ROWE: Well, Ben wrote Bob Jackson's opinion!

Even in foreign policy, I think I can get back to this business where you always rely, as most politicians do, on the men they knew in their youth. Roosevelt had his New Yorkers, Johnson had his Texans, Jimmy Carter had his Georgians—maybe he shouldn't have had them, but he had them. On foreign policy, I think that Roosevelt relied mostly on Sumner Welles and Ambassador Philips. They had been young Foreign Service career fellows when he was in town as assistant secretary of the Navy. I think, mostly, he listened to them. He did it, sort of surreptitiously because Cordell Hull was a great power with the Senate, and he didn't want to get crossed with him. Some of his cabinet members were sort of independent barons, Jesse Jones and Cordell Hull. These people he listened to on foreign policy were people like Sumner Welles and Bill Philips, people he had known a long time.

NARRATOR: I'm sure I speak for all of you in thanking Mr. Rowe. He's not only illuminated our understanding, but through his wit and good spirit he's lit up this whole room as is rarely done. We appreciate it very much.

POLITICAL LEADERSHIP AND THE ROOSEVELT PRESIDENCY

Thomas G. Corcoran

NARRATOR: We are very happy to welcome this group to a Forum with one of our most distinguished visitors. Thomas G. Corcoran is a graduate of Brown University and Harvard Law School with a Doctor of Laws from Harvard University. He was clerk to Supreme Court Justice Oliver Wendell Holmes, counsel to the Reconstruction Finance Corporation, assistant secretary of the Treasury, and special assistant to the attorney general. He was the major draftsman of some of the great historic legislation of modern times, the Security Act of 1933, the Federal Housing Act of 1933, the Federal Security Exchange Act of 1934, and a host of other vital and crucial legislation.

However, none of this quite captures as vividly as does a passage concerning the role and the personality in government of Mr. Corcoran in the crucial days of the 1930s. The author of *The Second Hundred Days: Franklin Roosevelt and the New Deal* writes, "Corcoran was a new political type, an expert who not only drafted legislation but maneuvered it through the treacherous corridors of Capitol Hill. Two Washington reporters wrote of him, 'He could play the accordian, sing any song you cared to mention, read Aeschylus in the original, quote Dante and Montaigne by the yard, tell an excellent story, write a great bill like the Securities Exchange Act, prepare a presidential speech, tread the labrythian mass of palace politics, or chart the future course of a democracy with equal ease. He lived with Ben Cohen and five other New Dealers in a house on R Street. As early as the spring of 1934 GOP congressmen were learning to ignore the sponsors of New Deal legislation and level their attacks on the scarlet fever boys from the little red house in Georgetown.'"

Those of us who have listened, even for a few minutes, to the political insights of Mr. Corcoran know that his verve and the energy reflected in the historical accounts persist into the present. We find it a great privilege to have him with us this afternoon to discuss political leadership, Franklin D. Roosevelt, perhaps Lyndon B. Johnson, with some reference to President Ronald Reagan.

MR. CORCORAN: You know, I was once a secretary to the Supreme Court and they used to say to the applicant before the Court, "Why are you here?" And you're supposed to say, "I'm appealing from the Fifth Circuit." Why am I here? I'm here because my junior partner, Jim Rowe, of whom I am a protege, was here with you last time and he asked me to come down here and finish saying in my imprudent way what he didn't say in his prudent way.

I'd like to talk for just a few minutes before I answer questions. I know that Jim Rowe would tell you I'm a hopeless romantic. But, I believe there is a connection between the administration of FDR and Lyndon B. Johnson and Mr. Reagan. My father used to say—my father was a Democrat and my mother was a Republican—that a child who doesn't take the politics of his father and the religion of his mother is either a victim of child abuse or he is a filial ingrate. So I am a Democrat.

And I am a Democrat for Reagan for one reason. There is one thing, one very essential reason why Roosevelt and Reagan are very alike. I think Mr. Reagan, whatever he says about what he is going to do about the Social Security Act or the tax bill or anything else, has had the same effect that Franklin Roosevelt and Lyndon Johnson had in unleashing the energies of the million of Americans in this country who, by the very unleashing, will pull the country through, despite what a given piece of legislation is. Note the recent polls on the country's increasing optimism.

I wasn't a Roosevelt man when I first came in. I had been legal secretary to Mr. Justice Holmes. As such I came to Washington in 1926 with Calvin Coolidge. I remember the Teapot Dome scandal. And I had been in the New York District Attorney's office in the prosecution of Harry Dougherty. I had a very low opinion of what went on in government. But I was an employee of the Court; I was tied up with the Court.

The first president I ever met was Calvin Coolidge. I had to work my way through law school and spent the summers working on a fishing trawler out of Boston, fishing the Georges Banks. Consequently, I knew the waist, bust and hips of every fish in the North Atlantic. By Mr. Holmes, I was taken to the Judicial Reception at the White House to meet Mr. Coolidge.

Now Mr. Coolidge was a fellow who conserved energy. When he shook hands with you, he just held out his hand and your hand was supposed to slide off of it. By the time I got to the end of the line his hand was rather sweaty. My first impression of a President of the United States was "haddock."

When people say to me, "Why are you for Mr. Reagan?" I say, "That's like the question, Do you love your wife? Compared to whom? He is here, isn't he? Who else is Commander-in-Chief?" In 1927, I went from Justice Holmes to Wall Street. Things were very prosperous at that time. But the old Justice who was a very wise man who had watched the Harding administration and its trouble, said, "Son, we're only in the eye of a hurricane. There is another side coming."

I landed in Wall Street just in time to see the boom and the bust. But I was very fortunate. I went with a very small office, not one of these big ones which I don't believe in. My office was made up of partners who had been in the Wilson administration during World War I and they all were followers either of Wilson or Teddy Roosevelt. All had been either in the Progressive Movement or they had been with McAdoo of the Treasury. All were very interested in what was going on in Washington.

So, although they taught me to be a good Wall Street lawyer, these men were always interested in how the government was working. And I must say that I found out when I went back to Washington when I was working with Roosevelt, there were more good Wall Street men and more good Republicans than you can believe who helped and were willing to help Roosevelt.

Returning to Washington in March, 1932, I was over for one year with Hoover as a lawyer in his Reconstruction Finance Corporation because my boss, who was Mr. Franklin of the Baltimore family and a former assistant secretary of the Treasury, couldn't come down to help and my other boss, Joseph Cotton, had already come down as under secretary of state for Hoover to try to pull us through the Manchurian crisis. So I was the only bachelor in the office; there was a call for somebody to come down and help Mr. Eugene Myer, then head of the Federal Reserve, later the head of the *Washington Post*. So I came down to help the bi-partisan RFC in the banking crisis for a whole year with Hoover before Roosevelt came in. In those days a president was inaugurated in March, not in January. So because my bosses couldn't come with the trouble on the Street, I came down in March of 1932 to help all the banks a full year before Roosevelt's actual inauguration.

In those days, maybe like you, I was a great Walter Lippmannite. And Walter Lippmann had a very poor opinion of Roosevelt as the Governor of New York. He was then going through the Jimmy Walker problem with that lovely Betty Compton girl, and the Seabury Investigation. Lippmann, whom I then followed religiously as an intellectual out of Harvard Law School and a teaching fellow in the Harvard Law School, had a very low opinion of

Roosevelt. "Remember," he said, "The only qualification Roosevelt has is he is a nice man and he wants to be elected." I left New York just as Roosevelt was in that trouble with Seabury and Walker.

Now in 1932 the RFC itself was in trouble because both the Democrats and the Republicans did their damnedest to keep it in trouble. The Reconstruction Finance Corporation made loans on collateral to banks. But the Democrats, in order to beat Hoover, insisted that every loan to the bank had to be publicly reported. If you were a depositor in a little bank down South and you read in your paper that the bank had to borrow and borrow from the government, what would you do? You would pull your money out.

On the other hand, poor old Hoover, for whom I had great personal respect, had a secretary of the treasury named Ogden Mills succeeding Andrew Mellon who by this time had left to be Ambassador to Great Britain. At that time, the Treasury under the law as changed under Roosevelt had to put up the money for the RFC. Later the RFC, under Jesse Jones for whom I worked eight years, had separate appropriations. Mills was anti-government spending and he wouldn't let the RFC spend too much money. Mills was a very strong and able man in his beliefs belonging to the old Wall Street barons who in previous depressions used to wait until everything went to pot and go down and buy Wall Street out cheap. This time the country refused to let that happen and by November, 1933, Hoover was not elected.

Now all through the summer of 1933 we knew in the RFC and the Treasury what we had to do to bail out the banks to stay bailed out. Mr. Hoover tried to see Mr. Roosevelt to talk with him about it. But, for complicated reasons I could not understand at that time, Mr. Roosevelt wouldn't see Mr. Hoover. So for six months the RFC and the bank failures went along and things got worse and worse until the big bank in Detroit blew up; Detroit is always the boom and bust point of our economy. When Mr. Roosevelt was inaugurated, he had to close the banks the next day.

What then did I think of Mr. Roosevelt? Of course, at that time I had only a Wall Street lawyer/banker's mind, although I was later to be Mr. Roosevelt's assistant secretary of the treasury. Then I thought it was outrageous for Mr. Roosevelt to let the banks go under when we knew what to do—which we did do after the Hundred Days. I honestly suspected he planned it that way for political reasons.

I always remember my problem of conflict of interest at that time. I had come out of an old seafaring family. The rule of the old sailing ships was "When you go up in the rigging and it's bad, one hand for yourself, one hand for the ship." So, I went down to the only bank that was alive and I drew only half my money out and put it in my pocket. "One hand for myself." I left the other half in for the ship. This solved my conflict of interest standing up before Mr. Roosevelt as he made that famous speech at the Inaugural, safe no matter which way it came out. But I honestly didn't believe that Mr. Roosevelt would make it.

Later that week when I could get an appointment, I went to see Justice Holmes to say, "Mr. Justice, I am going back to New York. Because I am only a junior member of that outfit in New York—it is a wonderful one—if I stay here much longer, I'll lose my place."

But my old friend, Felix Frankfurter said, "Did you know that I have seen Roosevelt?" Now Felix was a very clever fellow. He had known Roosevelt when they both were in the War Department in the old Theodore Roosevelt administration. Very cleverly, he outflanked Lippmann. There was a god higher than Lippmann to us liberals and it was Justice Holmes. So about the third day of Roosevelt's incumbency, Felix managed to get Roosevelt to call on Holmes. That outflanked Mr. Lippmann completely.

So when my farewell speech was delivered, the old Justice said, "Well, you know more than most about this bank business and, son, we are in trouble. You know it didn't make any difference to me when I was a captain in the Civil War whether it was Burnside or Hallack or Mead who was commander-in-chief. Now Roosevelt's commander-in-chief." There is a story that as Roosevelt left the Holmes' library, Holmes saluted him as captain to commander-in-chief. That's the way I think about Reagan.

Holmes ended with, "Son, we are in trouble. You can make up your mind about your future, but I would think you would want to stay around to see if you can help. You know, he's Teddy Roosevelt again. He may be a second class intellect, boy, but he is a first class temperament and that's what counts in a president. Because if he awakens the people, their own efforts as individuals will be enough to pull the country through no matter what he does." The Justice's prophecy about FDR following TR was true.

So I went back to work for a new RFC and I have been doing something around Washington ever since.

You know, we went through the Hundred Days. Much of its legislative approach never lasted. It was being changed and revised all the time Roosevelt was in office. But what was important was that he did fire up the country. He got it off its despair. And he adopted almost verbatim—because he had no platform of his own except to balance the budget—the old Progressive Party platform of Robert La Follette which was then represented by George Norris and Burt Wheeler who had come over to Roosevelt. It was the old TR Progressive platform which brought in the Tennessee Valley Authority, the Housing Acts and the Securities Act, and all the rest of what is called the New Deal. Franklin Roosevelt really adopted the whole Teddy Roosevelt program.

My first friend in Washington had been Dean Acheson. Dean

had been the clerk to Brandeis before I was the clerk to Holmes, and Dean had another, a senior partner, who had been the Teddy Roosevelt organizer in Chicago named Edward Burling. Burling had a place up on the Potomac River of about four hundred acres where he hosted an unofficial seminar up there of all the old Bull Moose crowd. There I first met Hiram Johnson and Harold Ickes. Another one into the RFC as general counsel and my boss, Stanley Reed, who later became a Justice of the Supreme Court. Reed was a very important fellow in the whole Roosevelt administration. He came from a rich Kentucky agricultural family who had gone to Columbia Law School and the Sorbonne. He understood perfectly well that as Roosevelt poured in his progressive ideas, you had to have government servants who understood money. He asked me—I had been the New York recruiting agent for Harvard Law School—to find men for the RFC.

That's when there began to run into the Roosevelt administration the all-important first thousand men down. The number one of the cabinet and the number two of the cabinet are important. But without these thousand guys under numbers one and two, the nameless fellows in subordinate positions that provide the energy for the top men who had to go to political parties or home to their wives at night, you don't get driving power in any administration. Reed told me, "Find me men." Then, first with help from Franklin in New York and Felix, I began to find men.

Now you take Jim Rowe. Jim was the last secretary to Justice Holmes. I had been, myself, ten years before. Jim and I were with Justice Holmes when he died. I put Jim in the RFC as one of its lawyers. I met Ickes at Burling's. I told Ickes about Jim. Jim transferred to the Interior where Ben Cohen was. After the Securities Act, Jim went to the SEC, then to the Labor Department. When after the 1936 election, the president's staff was regularized, Jim became an administrative assistant to the president, then deputy attorney general until he went to war.

Jim Rowe was only a type. What others complained was an "underground railroad" that put Jim Rowe in the U.S. Government completely revitalized that government. Imagine the "institutionalization of compassion," as we used to call it. Think of what Harry Hopkins had to do all over this country finding somebody in every country, in every city to do something that had never been done before. Remember there was no welfare abuse (or even welfare itself) in the Roosevelt administration, no government inflation, no government debt. And everybody who could work had to work for something called "jobs." At the beginning we had to find some lousy stuff to call work, but at the end, work was on bridges and tunnels and highways and airports. And for those who couldn't work, Roosevelt, with the energy of his young helpers created Social Security.

All this time, until he died, I was talking to Justice Holmes about government in the history of the U.S. Holmes didn't die for three years after Roosevelt had come in. Jim and I were always talking to him about what was happening to the administration. He backed Roosevelt but he was always thinking. He told me something which in one way particularly found favor with Roosevelt. He said, "You know what really matters in the politics of this democratic country? Did you ever see a circus parade come down the streets of Salem, Massachusetts?"

"No."

"When the circus parade is formed back where they get off the train, the elephants are in front of the parade. As the elephants move into the central part of the city, little boys come out from the side streets to strut in front of the elephants and pretend they are leading the parade. But if they should turn down a side street, the elephants will keep going where they intended to go in the first place."

"And what are the elephants?"

"Elephant number one is the resources of the country. Call it geography. What have you got? Oil, metal. Development of resources.

"Elephant number two is people. Call it demography. What kind and how many people—their living depends on its resources."

Think of our demographic-resource problem now. The last census shows we are moving from the resource-emptied cities of the North—New York and Cleveland, everything except my state of New Hampshire which has no taxes—moving even out of the cities along the American Mediterranean, which is our Great Lakes, because everything really was based on a steel economy—from resources of coal, limestone and iron.

But the present projected economy is from oil, sulphur and water, and it's moving right down to the Southwest and the South. The Democratic party, my party has got to understand that, no matter what my friend Teddy Kennedy says. The last census shows the movement of the country is out of the Northeast and out of the Midwest to the Southwest and the South, the places where the resources of energy and chemistry are running the economy and therefore the politics of the country.

That's what I think Reagan is about and Wall Street knows it. I make no bones about it and I have great respect for the fellows on Wall Street. I know you can be a Wall Street lawyer Democrat. During the period when Roosevelt was trying to get his things through the Congress in the Hundred Days and in the days thereafter when we had to redo what he wanted, there were more decent helpers out of Wall Street and the Republican party than are assumed. I remember particularly Robert Lovett, Paul Shields, James Forrestal, Stanley Reed, James Wadsworth, Carl Mapes.

The Roosevelt government was, in truth, a government of unity. For myself I have never cared much—and much less than Jim—what the politics of anybody was as long as he would work and deliver, with others going his way. That's where I hope we are now.

Back to Justice Holmes' elephants. The third elephant is technology. When my brother was with General Motors in Tokyo there was nothing but American cars on the road all the way to Bangkok. Now we're struggling to keep American cars on the roads of the United States. My brother went out with General Motors in the hopeful export era in the dream of Hoover, Secretary of Commerce. He came back in about eight years when he saw coming the invasion of Manchuria by Japan. Lately he said to me, "You know what happened when I pulled out of GM? There was a fellow named Toyota working for me in the trucking department. I noticed how interested he was in the trucks. The minute the Japs went into Manchuria, the first thing that happens is that Grandfather Toyota emerged in charge of the provision of trucks from the GM factory for the Japanese Army's invasion of Manchuria." We have given away our technology.

We were very generous to Europe in the Marshall Plan and to Asia in Japan. And we put plants into places where there is a lower wage rate with our technology and where there is a kind of society which more easily takes government's orders. Our research, even biological research, is in many fields perilously behind Japan and Germany and France, the Middle East; and God knows if the OPEC nations keep piling their money into technological education and production . . .

Getting for a moment into the ERA and women's lib, a very intelligent lady congressman who I think really saved Voyager and the Shuttle is Mrs. Hale Boggs. She once laughed at me, "Do you know where women's lib began? Not with male politicians. It began with the invention by man of the sewing machine so women didn't have to make the family clothes anymore. You know where it got its next push? With the telephone. The telephone girl was the first to get out in the commercial world. She had nice clothes and she was the first woman who ever made a wage. And after that you know what you made for us? The typewriter. It was just exactly the socio-political effect of the invention of the cotton gin and its relation to the War between the States."

By accident, I was on the edges of the atom bomb. We were six months behind Hitler, but I remember a remark of Harold Urey who died not so long ago—the fellow who brought Niels Bohr to the United States: "You know, we are six months behind. There are only four men, probably, in England, and in Germany and the United States who understand the theory of this fission. But we're going to get there first because we have so many thousand more steamfitters and electricians.'' We locked them up in Hanford, Washington, and we produced it. Whether we have unforeseen consequences from that invention is beside the point here.

One thing that always interested me about the war was how much we won with brains and productivity and not with bayonets. How did we pull off the invasion of the Pacific? With Kaiser's assembly line product of ''tinships.'' We were turning them out ten a day.

The war in the Atlantic? With a Pole's help we broke the German code as well as the Japanese. We did it with accelerated technology and we can do it again. Maybe I am an enthusiastic romantic but I honestly believe with this third elephant, technology, we can get ahead again. The boys at Massachusetts Institute of Technology and the boys down in NASA, which Lyndon Johnson set up as the counterpart to MIT, tell me that if we would really want energy hard enough, as we wanted that atom bomb hard enough, we could have hydrogen fusion maybe in even three, but no more than five years, instead of twenty. That would end dependence on foreign energy that we have causing inflation all over the world.

What interests me about what's going on now is that I think the point is that Mr. Reagan understands the elephants. I watched Mr. Reagan work once when he was to eliminate the communists in the Hollywood unions. Not so long ago, after I had lost on another candidate, because I can't keep my cotton-picking fingers out of this business, I talked with him.

''Do you remember when I worked on the Hollywood unions?''

''Yes.''

''Just remember, Governor Reagan, that when you were getting that done you were both a Democrat and a union leader. There are not enough Republican registered voters. The old Roosevelt liberals that have become conservatives as we built up the middle class are the voters you have to reach. Don't say anything against Franklin Roosevelt.''

Did you notice his speech accepting his nomination? At the Inaugural? He's just like Roosevelt. He's just like Teddy Roosevelt, as Holmes said. And Justice Holmes had his differences with Teddy Roosevelt. Homes voted against his president's wishes on the dissolution of the North Pacific Railroad and Roosevelt said he could cut ''a judge with more backbone out of a banana.'' They didn't invite the Justice to the White House for a while. But, the president came around.

Again, about the manpower in government. What I am thinking about these days is that unfortunately as a result of the abuses of the Nixon administration, we overdid the thing of reforming the relationship between the Executive Branch and the Congress. With the best intentions Common Cause did it. For instance, Mr. Reagan is out there today trying to find people who will take cabinet positions which require being picked over for peccadillos by senators seeking fame. You saw the other day the "revelation" of Justice Lewis Powell's worth that he had five million dollars worth of real estate and that Chief Justice Burger had a million dollars worth of real estate. I am even wondering about ABSCAM. I am telling you we went through all of this business with the best intentions. But I wonder whether we've gotten to the point where it has become almost dangerous for an able man, if he has a wife and children he cares about, to run for Congress or to take a government job.

I was lucky enough, with Jim Rowe as an example and helper, to help energize Roosevelt's administration when it had to take on this enormous job of government helping on everything when there was nobody else to help. But suppose you are now a young fellow at my age at that time—Jim was a little younger—you had a family and children and you are asked to move to Washington. It would cost you three or four thousand dollars in a private school to put a child in the third grade which you'd feel you had to do because if you came to live in Washington you'd find a particular public school system that you'd hesitate to put your children in. You'd also find costs sky-high and no place to rent. The reason isn't only inflation. It's because anybody who ever came to this lovely city of Washington never wants to leave it. No wife would let you. And I don't blame her. It's one of the most lovely towns for a woman to live in this world. Maybe Virginia is, I don't know. So what are these young people going to do?

If you are a congressman it is too dangerous to raise your salary. If a congressman raises his salary, he may get beaten for that. So you can't get people in Washington of the kind it was easy to get in Roosevelt's day. It's generally assumed that the cabinet Mr. Reagan has now is not made up entirely of his first choices. He couldn't get a man, for instance, from Citibank because that bank has loans to the Third World guaranteed by the government. It is said he couldn't get his first choice for secretary of the Interior because his choice had sons who run cattle on government-owned land in what is called a conflict of interest. I think first we've got to stop being so anti-system or you can't run a government of such enormously complicated responsibilities. And second, we have to raise the congressional salaries to $80,000 so we can get some young fellows to work all night to energize this government at a comparable lower salary.

Now something else. Roosevelt always was interested in the Pacific. When the war came, few were interested in the Pacific among his crowd but me. Why? Because of my brother and my senior New York partner, Mr. Joseph Cotton, under secretary of state, who had placed me in Hoover's administration. So, the White House asked me, eight months before Pearl Harbor, to help on the job of putting into the American Lend-Lease Plan—possibly in violation of the Neutrality Act—the U.S. aviation personnel of the Flying Tigers that went into China with General Chennault to help keep China from surrendering to Japan. I have watched that Pacific situation ever since.

Whatever happens in Europe, it is no use kidding yourself about China. I have stayed with this China interest for a long while and I am saying I think Reagan sees it clearly, even though Haig is going to go to Peking next month. These Chinese people, all of them, hold the lever of my grandchildren's America, even maybe of my children's America of the future, and your children's and grandchildren's America too. If you study what happened in China over the years when their once stabilized society was destroyed by European commercialization, they would have had a terrible hundred years of famine, warlords, foreign concessions, revolutions, and everything else. Too many people for their country, they haven't had enough to eat. They've had famines, no medical facilities and died like flies in infancy. What now remains is based on the Darwinian law of the survival of the fittest, the physically and mentally toughest people on earth.

When I quit at the end of the war, and I was working at the time with the Chinese, we were all saying goodbye. A fellow who was number two to T. V. Soong, both Foreign Minister and Ambassador to the United States, was my special friend. His name was Reichman. I had known him before the war as the head of the children's program of the League of Nations. "Tommy, are we always going to be friends?" I said, "Certainly." He said, "Are you sure? Do you know I'm number three in Polish Communist Intelligence? Come on over to Warsaw with me and see the future." Well, of course I said, "No." He went on, "I will give you one piece of advice and I am not salting the mine. Have you watched the Chinese under a bombing?"

"Yes."

"No matter how little they have to eat and how badly they have been banged up they sit down at night and enjoy what little they have and make merry. The Chinese are a bright-minded people. But did you ever hear a joke in India?"

"No. "

"The Indians are a dark-minded people. But you foolish Americans are going to take the dark-minded people for your choice and let us communists take over the bright-minded people."

Which is exactly what we did.

Now what are we going to do? The Mainland Chinese are trying to turn around. Now there are five other Chinas which got out all the fellows who had any capacity of managing anything to keep their heads from being cut off in the revolution. They're in a Singapore China, a Malaya China, an Indonesia China, a Hong Kong China, a Taiwan China, and there is a China on the Mainland—and an American China.

I was with my old friend, Ben Cohen, last night. I tried to bring him down here. The difference between Ben and myself is that Ben remembers that his ancestors were the High Priests of Israel and he continues to believe in the infinite perfectability of man. Just a Catholic, I believe in original sin! I think I don't fool myself about people. So I say, you watch this China situation as the most important factor in your children's future. And how do you handle it? The Chinese, from their survival of the deprivations of that last hundred years, are such a money-minded people that they are born with an abacus in their hand. Maybe even Chiang Kai-shek must have realized that it was impossible to have two Marshall Plans. To get the Japs out of China, we had to knock them out by bombing, bombing, bombing everything in sight. There was nothing left to live on. But they survived. They are Chinese and they are patient.

One wonderful thing we did after the Boxer Rebellion was to take our indemnity and put it into a fund for sending Chinese students to the United States. Those students are in the five outside Chinas, particularly in Taiwan. And the Taiwan standard of living now is the second highest, to Japan, in the world. That wise Chinese mind on the Continent just keeping alive is thinking, "Why can't we live at that standard of living? Why can't we go to school? Why can't we have an automobile instead of a bicycle?" Keep the U. S. trained Chinese outside the Mainland alive and we have a chance that it, the Continent, will come out all right.

When we were having the Supreme Court Packing Plan which was a mess for everyone in it, for and against, the only candidate who spoke up for a congressional bi-election in Austin, Texas, was a young fellow named Lyndon Johnson. Of the nine candidates, everyone was against Roosevelt except Lyndon and split the anti-Roosevelt vote. Mrs. Johnson put up only ten thousand dollars to finance his campaign to pull him through. After the election when Roosevelt went down to Galveston on a cruiser, there he met Lyndon who had stuck up for him, and he brought Lyndon back on his train to Washington. Then he sent Lyndon to me for advice.

What mistakes they say Roosevelt and Johnson made were compensated by the great things they did. Johnson faced up to the Vietnam problem. I was associated with an airline which did the only air support at Dien Bien Phu because the French politicians in Europe forced us into it. They said: "We don't give a damn about Vietnam; we do care about the oil in Algeria. If we lose Vietnam, we lose Algeria. We mustn't lose Vietnam and you Americans must hold it for us." That's why I am worried about Mitterand; the way the French play us, "If you don't play with us and take care of Vietnam, we won't play with you in Europe." Long before Kennedy, long before Johnson, under Eisenhower, we were in Vietnam up to our necks to keep the French playing with us on the other side in Europe. Now don't blame Lyndon for it. Don't even blame Kennedy for it. This thing started under Eisenhower because France made us do their work. Lincoln crossed a great river preventing economic sectionalism from breaking up the Union. Roosevelt crossed the next great river preventing economic disaster in a poverty-frightened people from breaking up the Union. Lyndon crossed the next great river, preventing its being broken up under the strain of racial differences. Together they led a people always tempted to division to develop a tolerant huge middle class, the biggest national asset of ability and stability in history. No matter what else is said about Lyndon Johnson, maybe he created the beginning of the solution to the race problem; he crossed the widest river of all.

Back to our three elephants—the technology elephant. We have a real problem of technology. That is whether we are going to supplement, in time, the resources upon which our population explosion is putting pressure. That requires inventing new resources, whether it is hydrogen fusion or something like it. We have the demographic problem creating the pressure on resources.

My mother's father was a genuine Forty-Niner. Their motto was: "The cowards never started and the weak died by the way." My father, whose father was an immigrant, not a Forty-Niner, to get respite from my mother used to take me down to where the Fabre Line was bringing in Italian immigrants when I was a boy. He said, "Son, every infusion of immigration in this country has brought people who just as truly as your mother's Forty-Niners believe 'The cowards never started and the weak died by the way.' What keeps this country going is the constant refueling of ambition and the willingness to work of those people who are coming in." Now we are facing it. You have to either stretch your technology to have room to take new people in with their increased push on resources or you have to face up to turning them away. It is not only the problem from Mexico; it is the problem from the so-called boat people who are fundamentally of Chinese stock.

What I like about Mr. Reagan is that I think he thinks about Justice Holmes' elephants. I think he is capable of giving the American people hope rather than depressing them about their morale. As with Franklin Roosevelt, within one month he had transformed the whole attitude of individuals of this country. And re-energization of the able is the only chance we have got. I think if he plays it wisely, we Democrats should be smart enough to give him a break. I think he's transforming the country, and he isn't a political possession of his right wing.

I don't care whether idealogues consider him a "first-class intellect." The important thing that counts is temperament and whether he gives the able middle class hope. I think he will face the Chinese situation, the technological situation, the demographic situation. I think he will pull us up to number one in this resource war.

When Holmes talked about how Roosevelt was doing, he said, "You know, he first understood and acted accordingly that the biggest waste of assets of the country is unused labor." What was the first thing that he did with the CCC Camp? He developed resources and he put the unemployed young to work. If we wanted what we want hard enough, we could do it today. For three years I have been asking "What is the easiest CCC equivalent of taking care of the forest now?" I think it's rebuilding the railroad roadbeds of our whole system on a freight basis no matter who owns the damned things. But the unions won't let you do it. The maintenance men say, "You mean you are going to put these kids in to redo these tracks? What's left for us?" And my reply is, "Well, I favor our laboring man. I worked on the Fair Labor Standards Act but I say, Mr. Maintenance, if you don't let this rehabilitation of the railroads happen, there isn't going to be anything for you to do ten years from now as we go ahead at building truck roads and barge lines and air freight airports." On the other hand, there is no way in the world to move goods cheaper than a steel wheel on a steel rail.

I think Reagan knows as a politician he has to try to keep promises, but he was a wise governor. Like Roosevelt when he knows a first plan can't make it, he is going to find a way to change his mind. The important thing to understand is you are never sure of how anything is going to work out when you begin. I don't like to talk to these intellectuals who think you can deal with politics as abstract ideology. Everything is the next untried cake of ice.

Roosevelt used to say, "Did you ever see a smart engineer start a long train of coal cars? Do you think he eases the throttle in? He jerks it to beat the inertia." Do you remember Eliza in *Uncle Tom's Cabin* trying to get across the frozen, iceloaded Ohio River to freedom? Certainly Eliza had in mind the freedom on the other side of the Ohio, a free state. But what she was thinking of immediately was the next cake of ice. What bothers me about intellectual critics is their disregard that the immediate problem is always the next cake of ice. Reagan must know cutting back social security was a mistake. Did you ever think maybe as a politician, he had to let the Democrats win that so if he let them win on the social security business, he might do better on his tax bill?

Once in 1936 I travelled on campaign with Mr. Roosevelt just as someone to help cut down speeches. My only value was that I boiled a hundred twenty minutes into twenty. One day we were in southern Illinois. We were whistle-stopping and at every whistle stop, the president would reward the head of the delegation cheering at the stop with the courtesy of riding to the next whistle stop, then similarly taking on the next head of delegation. When we finally sat down to work on the speech, he said, "Did you learn anything today?" I said, "I was puzzled, Mr. President. You know I am a lawyer and I think in very accurate, specific terms. Now, Mr. President, you let me listen today while you were talking with those men." This was southern Illinois. "Everyone of them wanted to be assistant secretary of agriculture." He said, "Yes, that's right." I said, "But you talked to them in such a way that every one of them went off the train thinking you had literally promised it." He said, "That's right."

"Well, who is going to get it?"

"The ambitious man that makes the most trouble if he doesn't get it."

That's politics.

QUESTION: I have a question about Social Security. Back in 1934 or 1935, Leon Keyserling who then was Robert Wagner's secretary, asserts that the Social Security Bill could have been and should have been passed in 1934. Because FDR appointed a committee and because of Elizabeth Brandeis' sort of silly objection, it came in 1935. It was obviously going to come. Even *Fortune,* in February of 1935, said, "The question is not whether there will be a Social Security Act; the only question is when?" Now why did FDR postpone it from 1934 until the next year?

MR. CORCORAN: Well, I don't know what went into the calculations of that incredibly skillful political mind. As I remember, we were in a lot of trouble in 1934, a lot of money trouble. That was about the time we were running into the NRA, wasn't it? And of course he took these things when he could. It took some time. Miss Perkins was always working on that and Ben was working on it and Leon was working on it. I wasn't working on it, but I remember at that time we were having a lot of trouble and we passed the Social Security Act because of the Townsend business, remember? Huey Long was pushing us around at that time to share the wealth. Maybe at that time, the time of the congressional elections, we were surprised when we won more than we ever expected. Maybe we just had too much to worry about. You know a fellow who is sitting up there has to balance what you can get done with what you've got.

QUESTION: The next cake of ice?

MR. CORCORAN: The next cake of ice.

QUESTION: I was much taken with the phrase "the institutionalization of compassion" when you were discussing the recruiting of the thousand middle-level administrators that were needed. Many of us have the impression that the people recruited now are not to make the government work but to prevent it from functioning, particularly in terms of regulations. Would you comment on this?

MR. CORCORAN: Well, it is for a reason, as I told you. You take Joe Califano. Joe, you know, is writing now about his troubles in HEW and Joe deliberately picked HEW because, being responsible for that incredible operation in Lyndon's time, he wanted to prove it could work. But, you know, it won't work for this reason. The minute you get into the situation where you are giving something away, you find political pressures from the people who want something from you to take over the organization of the thing. There is a great difference between the kind of thing like the SEC where you are stopping people from acting and the kind where you are giving something to people. They try to take over. Right now, you people are intellectuals. You deliberately organized the Department of Education in order to get a racket, didn't you? Why do you think all the teachers were for Carter the last time? So they could organize the Department of Education that the National Association of Teachers could run. So what you have got to do is sit down and see whether you can get enough people who are willing to take the rap and be sure to be fired in two years. I quit when I knew I was going to be fired.

QUESTION: As one of the very practical matters, what is going to be done by Reagan about the arms race?

MR. CORCORAN: Well, remember I represent Newport News Shipbuilding Company, but I can tell you one thing very clearly. There is too much tempting fat in the defense procurement process. Now, I am going to talk from my own problem. You saw this business over in General Dynamics on the submarines, didn't you? And you saw the accusations made? For an awful long time—because I was in that row with Admiral Rickover—my crowd down here in Newport News would not bid on an undesigned ship like the Trident. But General Dynamics and everybody else was deliberately bidding below what they knew it would cost to get the contract. Then half way through they'd say, "You have to do better by us or we aren't going to deliver."

Now the first thing my friend, Secretary of Defense Weinberger, has to do is take the fat out. Some contractors are milking that Defense Department. The second thing that he has got to do is face up to the fact that you are going to have—I don't care whether you academics like it—a draft in two years because the trouble is that you are building weapons beyond the capacity of the fellows you've got to man them.

The other day, the former head of the Marines, General Walt, said to me, "You know, we have more computerized artillery. But I am telling you, if a shell should hit the computer, we couldn't lay in a gun." There is no use fooling yourself.

I'm concerned when I see all these children turning their backs on speeches about defense and the rest of it. It's the same old racket. The real trouble in the last war, and the trouble with the whole Defense Department theory, is that we are letting the children that want to go to college be excused from being in the Army and their girlfriends are raising holy hell about human rights; and all of it to keep them from going into the service.

Another thing you would want to do is to pay enough money to keep the defense personnel that are good and are leaving by the dozens. The rest of them are going off on these atomic submarines we build at Newport News and having all that trouble with their wives raising hell because they are out for six months. You are going to have to take care of them. I am telling you that you are going to have a draft in two years, and that's going to be a lot of political fun.

QUESTION: I agree with your emphasis on temperament being important. That's why Lincoln was a great president and Roosevelt was a great president and Johnson said what he said about "we shall overcome." What is there in Reagan's temperament that suggests that he could be a compassionate person? And how would this compassion be institutionalized? How will he take the next step? Temperament determines the way we respond to the next problem. What is there about his temperament that would suggest a compassionate man?

MR. CORCORAN: Well, I want you to notice, in the first place, he did get elected. And Sam Rayburn once told me that a fellow who is effective as a politician basically had to be analyzed by his followers as a warm lively man. It is the sense of that quality about him on the part of the public that makes his communication with them acceptable. And Reagan is a great communicator and he knows how to fudge, if you don't mind my saying so. In some ways, he is an amazing man to me. I was Adlai Stevenson's classmate and I was in Adlai's campaign. Compare Reagan's success with Stevenson's defeat. It is an amazing thing that a candidate who had a divorce and who has a daughter who is marrying a guy ten years younger than herself and a son who was sending out ads for his business, should get away with it. You could no more have gotten away with that ten years ago than the man in the moon. You wouldn't have put up a divorced man. What I am saying is I feel very much that he senses what you have to do to stay in office and that's to be felt as human by his followers.

Now one more thing. I don't think the fellow wants to stay in for more than four years. He knows how he wants to leave this thing. I believe he believes in the simple things, the family, for instance, even though he has had a divorce and he has had lots of problems. I think he understands compassion and I think he understands spending money for which you get value. But it means something else. It means getting the kind of men, even from Wall Street if you dare to, who can run an organization. I know Joe Califano. I said, "Joe, what happened in HEW?" He said, "You couldn't keep special interest politics out of it."

Now I think Reagan has strengths. He is seventy years old; I am eighty years old. And old age ain't for sissies, even if you are seventy. I think the very fact that this president is seventy years old means that he is going to try to get this thing cleaned up before he finishes, and he's not going to run for office again. I have seen more trouble with men wanting to run for office forever. I am not sure, having watched the operation of politicians for a long time, but that social security is something he let them propose to be objected to and then he gave in.

At the same time, you have this business about the budget. Of course, you have to think about the budget, but also, think about how with spending we created, from a poverty-stricken nation, a middle class. I think it is a good thing to put some pressure on the middle class because now it has cars and television. I remember when we were playing with garbage cans. The middle class has children in college. It still wants those things so badly that it will work to keep them and it can take a little squeeze. I keep saying to you, the thing to do is to get the individual human animal in the United States to want, to want, to want it hard enough to work for it. I think Roosevelt did that. I think Lyndon did it. I think Reagan is going to do it. And, besides, I keep thinking so because there ain't nobody else to do it.

QUESTION: Well, I have a most unintellectual question. I have been fascinated most about you talking about Mr. Ickes, whom I remember vaguely. I used to get a good chuckle out of reading him. In the 1940 presidential campaign—you were talkng about the 1936 campaign—I seem to remember that the phrase that you used was used very effectively with a little addition to it by Mr. Ickes against Wendell Wilkie. Wasn't Mr. Ickes the one who said: "that poor, barefoot Wall Street lawyer?"

MR. CORCORAN: That's right.

QUESTION: Was that spontaneous or was that planned?

MR. CORCORAN: Ickes was one of the great underrated people of this country. Ben Cohen and I were his executors when he died.

Don't you fool yourself about Ickes. Old Ickes was the kind of guy that Roosevelt could always call on. You remember that old story about English tradition in old medieval England where, when a King was elected, a challenger had to ride on his horse armed "cap-a-pie" right into Westminister Hall, there to offer to challenge and fight to the death right there anybody who said the choice of King wasn't the rightful King. Well, Ickes was that challenger for Roosevelt. And he loved to do it except he used to talk too long. His speeches were an hour long.

But never mind. Whenever there was trouble old Ickes would ride in to be the attacker. Roosevelt would never say the sort of thing about Wilkie that Ickes said. Remember, Ickes was also the fellow who talked about Dewey as "the little fellow on the wedding cake." He had genius for this and he loved to do it.

QUESTION: Well, would he just snap them off or did he think?

MR. CORCORAN: No, he thought that way. You know, he was a very strange fellow. A lot of people thought he was a cantankerous old guy. But remember, Ickes came in with the Balinger controversy hanging over the Interior. Remember? Teapot Dome? The Interior was supposed to be a place where they stole money, and Ickes had to be a very cantankerous old guy who kicked people around to stop the stealing.

But there was another side to Ickes. He was a great botanist, like Thomas Jefferson. If you go to Washington today, you go down and look at that park in between the old Interior Building and the new one. It is one of the most beautiful little parks in the world, and Ickes was the fellow who built it. You go down and you stand in back of the Capitol and you look down the great sweep of "magnificent distance" down to the Lincoln Memorial and the Washington Monument. It wasn't there when I came here. There were railroad tracks that crossed between the Capitol. Ickes put the railroad tracks to Richmond underneath in a tunnel.

You know, when the war was coming on and we had to have the Pentagon in a hurry, a fellow named Somervell was a brigadier general there who had a great reputation for getting things done. He was ordered to build the Pentagon where the airfield was. So we had to have another airfield. The other airfield is today National Airport down on the Virginia side of the Potomac. We had to dig out the channel and make that airport with fill.

Burton Wheeler, at that time, was watching like a hawk for some indication that Roosevelt really wanted to get into the war. We had a specific limited appropriation for that airport. It was originally thought to be enough but Somervell spent so much money that in the middle of the summer of 1941, the money ran out. So Roosevelt called me in and he said, "I don't dare to ask for more money to finish the airport but we've got to have that money. Go around and see what discretionary appropriations cabinet members haven't expended yet that could be diverted into the airport. It might be a violation of the law but let's see what's available." I went around; I had to be very careful, but finally I saw our Ickes and I told him about Mr. Roosevelt's problem. Carefully, I didn't suggest what to do. Now, all I am going to say to you is that every time I land on Washington Airport and I hear the reverse thrust and the squeal of tires, I think I hear a protesting Navajo. That's the kind of a guy he was.

QUESTION: How many times did he resign?

MR. CORCORAN: Oh, about every two weeks. And he was right! Remember that bill about the reorganization of the government to turn Forestry over to the Interior to become the Department of Natural Resources? Roosevelt promised Ickes four or five times he would transfer that away from Wallace's Department of Agriculture to Ickes. But he never carried it out, because every time he tried the bureaucracy of the Forest Service went to Wallace and whined about it and Wallace didn't want to take it on. So he went back to Roosevelt and somehow he postponed it. Now this is, again, the operation of politics. Ickes had his mind on Forestry because Gifford Pinchot, who was Teddy Roosevelt's head of the Forest Service, had knocked Ickes over the way he ran the Department of Interior. When Mr. Ickes didn't get what he was promised, he resigned and then Roosevelt would send me around to talk sweet to Ickes—I'm all over Ickes' diary. I would talk to Ickes and say, "There are bigger things involved than this. Let's think about oil and let's think about the other things."

He was the first to think about today's oil difficulties. During the war when he first went in—remember the Hundred Days—there was so much oil being produced in Texas that we actually put a limitation on the amount of oil that could move across the state boundary. Ickes was in charge of this. He called it "hot oil."

We've managed this oil problem very badly, I think. First, under the "hot oil" New Deal policy, we discouraged U.S. production. Then when the war was over, discouraged imports. Ickes was the fellow who forced the Americans into that monopoly the British had in the oil fields in the Middle East. He sent me down to Texas about imports right after the war. He said, "These Middle Eastern potentates haven't sold their full production of oil because they can't. You go down and you talk to Murchison and say, 'Listen, why don't you fellows keep your oil. You can buy for ten bucks a barrel and let them make some money. You pour the surplus into salt mines and we will give you a tax rebate for the oil you keep in the ground.'" Maybe that's what we should have done. Of course, the U.S. producers were thinking about their bank loans they had to pay off. Since the banks wouldn't give in on their loans, the U.S. producers couldn't go along with Ickes. Maybe that's why we are in the mess we are in today.

Ickes was a great guy. He did more for this country than anybody can dream; and he was always in trouble. But the reason he was always getting things done was he would fight for them. Naturally, Franklin Roosevelt at the top hated trouble. Rather than for him to have to make a decision, if you had to raise enough hell, you'd get what you wanted. Now I know that you think this is a whale of a way to run a railroad. Churchill once said democratic government was the worst form of government except any other. It's a kind of government that's constantly meeting the next cake of ice. The ordinary citizen can't completely understand, but a president has to think over the long term sequences. He has to watch the elephants. In the meantime he has to make all kinds of compromises.

Do you remember the silver bloc? Senator Hayden of Arizona was jamming up the price of silver through twelve senators lined up in Montana, Arizona, Colorado, Nevada and New Mexico. As a New Englander I could talk to my fellow regionalists to say, "Why don't you gang up on these guys with your twelve senators? If they are getting all they are getting out of the twelve senators in the silver bloc, why don't we put twelve senators together?"

"Oh," they would say, "that wouldn't be honest." Well, the silver bloc got what they wanted and we in New England didn't. I am sorry but that's the kind of free government you've got.

Look at it right now. Did you see what Meaney's successor in the labor union said the other day? He said, "I am not going to worry about the Northeast. I know where production is coming from. I know where the plants are going to be, and where the synthetic fuel is going to be, and we're going to rape the natural resources of the West, and it's the finish of the West. We are going to put coal out there, and we are going to put oil out there and we are going to put metal out there. That's where the laborers want to be."

Now that's the way you think if you are a special interest group. Did you understand why such an effort was made to break the non-union situation down here at the shipyard in Newport News? It was because it was the biggest single employer of non-union labor in the South. Now all you nice people think, you know, that government is something that God told Moses to write on tablets of stone. Instead, you have a government that has to play this game of the next cake of ice—this cake of ice, that cake of ice—one off against the other. The wonderful thing that Roosevelt had was a sense of timing. He knew when to try and when to hold back.

Now, you ask, where are we? One thing you can say is that FDR remembered elephant number one and saved a lot of the resources of this country, including its labor. He made us resource conscious. On the other hand, we can say that he brought out discouraged people up from poverty into a confident middle-class status. That means they are now difficult to handle. It's not as easy as the old days when you said, "Follow me and I'll give you something to eat." Poor old Hoover, whom I really liked, tried with two chickens in every pot, but he couldn't deliver. He didn't know how to play little by little.

Did Lyndon lose the Vietnam War? Did Mr. Roosevelt lose his war? We fought that war to save the British Empire and it's in ruins because it now has neither the resources of raw materials nor the closed markets it had in the Commonwealth. The only thing it's got is North Sea oil and the Hong Kong markets. We didn't intend that. We didn't intend to substitute Russian—something worse than German—totalitarianism. We might have done something about the Germans. But we can't do anything with the Russians but just beat them, that's all.

But on the other hand you have to say FDR tried, as no one else ever did, to make a better world. Holmes used to say about Wilson and the United Nations, the League of Nations. "The goddamn fool, didn't he understand that when he was on this side of the water, he was a remote power and they were afraid of him. When he went over to Paris, he was just a human being to be lied to."

I don't pretend to know where we are coming out. I am only thinking about what we are going to do about defense. Only one thing is sure—we have to be strong.

What the Russians have is a society that doesn't represent their people any more than Mao represented the Chinese people. But, they know how to organize force. The simplest thing to organize is not a productive economy but military force. So they get by the way Ghenghis Khan used to get by, the way they did in Finland. They just threatened a productive society with physical force and took over its production just as they took the plants out of Germany and they took the plants out of Manchuria.

Well, we have got to face up to it. I think Reagan will be hitting the United States right where it is needed when he gets us to face up to it. So at eighty years old, I think it is going to be a wonderful time!

I shall report to my boss, Mr. Rowe, that I said the things he didn't dare to say because he may still run for office.

Thank you.

NARRATOR: You also can report that one man sitting at this table counseled me some months back, "Your Forums are fine but if you want a Forum on politics, you had better invite Tommy the Cork." That man is probably as pleased today as all of the rest of us are. Thank you for an unforgettable hour and a half of reflections on politics.

THE ROOSEVELT LEGACY
Franklin D. Roosevelt, Jr.

NARRATOR: I would like to welcome you to a Forum with Franklin Roosevelt, Jr. Neither he nor his subject needs much of an introduction, but I decided to divide the introduction with his good and close friend, Jack Royer, who is also a very active member of our committee of Associates of the Miller Center. Mr. Royer will say just a word about Mr. Roosevelt and then I will try to place it in the context of other Forums.

MR. ROYER: It is an honor for me to have the privilege of introducing Franklin. I have known Franklin for a long time. Of course, you know he graduated from Groton and Harvard and from the University of Virginia Law School in 1940. He was a congressman for six years and skipper of a destroyer in the South Pacific for about five years. He was undersecretary of Commerce during President Kennedy's term.

In closing I would like to say that I have heard that one of the only reasons he was ever able to graduate from the Law School here in Virginia was that his father came down and made the famous "stab in the back speech" at the University!

NARRATOR: One word about the subject. Some of you have noticed that we have had various speakers on the Roosevelt legacy in recent weeks, Thomas Corcoran, Jim Rowe and others. One of the baffling aspects of the present scene is that on the one hand, almost all the pundits and analysts tell us that the answers of the Roosevelt era have little, if anything, to do with the present-day problems. Yet, on the other hand, in the same breath they tell us that there is a line running from Roosevelt to Reagan in the approach to problems of urgent national interest. This was the message that Mr. Corcoran gave us earlier. It was also the testimony that was collected when the Miller Center did the presidential press conference study. Almost all the press corps and press secretaries we interviewed said the model for press conferences was Franklin Roosevelt and his conduct of press conferences. So, in a multitude of ways we seem to come back to the Roosevelt legacy, while in the same breath denying that it has any relevance for the present era. Maybe in the course of discussing this subject Mr. Roosevelt will help us understand this paradox a little better than we do at the moment.

Following his opening remarks, two of our most distinguished Roosevelt historians at the University, Provost David Shannon and Professor Norman Graebner, will pose some issues they consider most central to an understanding of the domestic and foreign policy of the Roosevelt administration. Mr. Roosevelt can choose to either address all the questions, some of the questions, or none of the questions as he sees fit. Then we'll move to your questions.

MR. ROOSEVELT: Thank you very much, Ken, and all of you for coming. I want to preface my remarks by saying that I am no academician nor do I consider myself an intellectual. But, I have lived, as all of us have, here in an incredible century of our country's history. The Roosevelt Library in Hyde Park, I think, has more scholars visiting that presidential library than all the other presidential libraries put together and I think for really one reason. My father's public career stretched from his first election to the state senate in 1910 to 1945. If you can think back through the isolation of this country, from a military point of view, the U.S. really had no significant voice in world affairs. At that point it was still a debtor nation. And it was through his life and then on through my mother's life—she died in 1962—that this country became what it is today, the leader of the free world, the most powerful military nation in the history of humanity. Some will disagree with that. But, it has been an incredible stretch of years.

I was born in 1914 and so I still remember the flavor which we had in World War I when we were still considered a small country but capable of enormous national effort as we did in World War I, our first great national effort in world affairs. And then, from there, of course, we have grown into what we are today. So, it has been a facinating period and my father and my mother played really remarkable roles during that evolution of our country.

I think Jack is probably entirely correct that the only reason that I graduated from law school was because of the "stab in the back speech" which was a very interesting little incident in itself. Coming down on the train to speak at the graduation ceremonies in 1940, the year I graduated from law school, the State Department had said that my father should not include that phrase in that speech. If you look at the original text of that speech at the library at Hyde Park, that phrase is crossed out but not very strongly. He told me afterwards he didn't reach his decision until he got to that point in the speech. As you remember Italy had just invaded southern France—the hand that held the dagger. When he got to that point the empathy between him and his audience at the graduation ceremonies was such that he decided to include it.

Of course that made headlines. The isolationist groups in the country immediately thought that he was practically throwing us into World War II—I will touch in a minute about the war years. It was a very dramatic event and I am not sure that it was not the reason why I graduated from law school. But, it certainly made our graduation here that year of 1940 probably one of the most memorable graduation ceremonies in the history of this great university.

When FDR became president you will recall that he quite studiously avoided working with the outgoing president during what was then a relatively long hiatus period from election day in November until March 4, 1933. I think—quite rightly—he decided that when he took office then his programs should start, although the country continued in its misery, unemployment kept growing, and more and more Wall Streeters kept joining the apple sellers on Wall Street. It was a desperate period, we recall, for those of you who go back as far as I do.

I think there were really two or three fundamental philosophies. He was a student of history. And, he was an amateur student of economics. He was fascinated by Keynes. Shortly after he became president, Keynes came over for an extended series of visits with FDR. He did believe in the Keynes theory of the times but he had serious questions. He recognized the advisibility of what was then called "pump priming," using the federal government's credit. It was about the only credit that was worth anything in 1933 since many states, and of course New York City, was bankrupt. But he was concerned about—Keynes and he had long discussions—about the other side of the Keynesian theory, that when the economy recovered and unemployment was down, the government should repay the debts it had incurred during the "pump priming" period. He was concerned that within a free society it would be very hard to do the retrenchments in government that would be necessary to make the Keynesian theory a workable theory. Of course, he was absolutely right. We have followed for many years one side of the Keynesian theory but we, as a nation, have never been strong enough—nor has the presidency and the Congress—to apply the restraints during the boom years of economic growth.

His approach to government was really twofold. One was the resolution of the economic national crisis, but equally important was his belief that the misery of people was caused, not by themselves, but by the system. In other words, their misery was something of which they had no control and led him into a doctrine or philosophy of encouraging trade unionism. It led to the temporary programs—and I am going to draw a very sharp distinction between his economic thinking, which was to put a floor under the economy, and these temporary programs. We can take, for example, the federal deposit insurance corporation, social security, unemployment insurance. Remember I did not use the word welfare. I'll come to that. These were putting a floor under the economy. The rest of the New Deal program was, in his concept, temporary emergency measures to meet the situation which he hoped would be resolved.

First the PWA; it didn't move fast enough. His pragmatism came to the fore and he started the WPA. I remember there was a lot of criticism of the WPA employing people to rake leaves. He said: "I would rather have them raking leaves and taking a check home at the end of the week, and buying their own groceries, and supporting their families, and maintaining their self respect than to be on the dole." This was a very fundamental philosophy of FDR. He did not believe in the dole, which we now call welfare. He believed in the work ethic. And that is a very, very important side of his philosophy of government.

The AAA was first thrown out by the Supreme Court and then brought back in a measure which was acceptable to the new Supreme Court. He really thought of that, also, as more or less, a temporary program which should fluctuate as the agricultural part of our economy needed the floor under prices. Of course, we know the mechanism has changed from time to time, but that program has continued. But again, he did not want it to be a guaranteed income for farmers. He believed that when they were making profits at world prices, they should have very little government support. So I think we have got to think of the New Deal as broken down into two sides. One was the putting of the floor under the economy; and the other was the temporary, emergency programs. He was a total pragmatist.

My mother was influenced during her early education at a school in England run by Mme. Souvestre who was a very close friend of many of the members of the then Fabian Society. She was much more of a Fabian Society socialist, if you want to call it that, than he was. He was a total pragmatist. He used to say that she was his eyes, his ears, and his legs. Her job was to go out—there's a famous cartoon in *New Yorker Magazine* of two coal miners down at the bottom of a coal mine with their lamps on their heads: "My God, Mrs. Roosevelt, what are you doing here?" She went everywhere. There was no part of this country where she didn't go and communicate. She was an important public relations side of my father's relationship to the voters, to the people. She was also a very good reporter. But, she saw things through her early political philosophy, which was essentially the Fabian Society connection.

She was much more concerned with the misery of people, quite bored with the economics of the country. So she was a prod to him on that side of the program, more of the emergency side.

She also had influence over other programs. The most striking example was when he started the CCC to take the kids off the streets and start teaching them some vocational skills, to become carpenters, plumbers, electricians and so on and so forth. An enormous amount of conservation was done by the Civilian Conservation Corps, the CCC. She didn't like the fact that FDR, in his pragmatic way, had brought back members of the national guard and the military reserve who were unemployed and given them jobs as the leaders of the CCC camps. He was putting men back to work, leading kids off the streets, but she didn't like the military overtones of the CCC. So she lobbied hard and finally got the National Youth Administration which became an umbrella for everything from young artists and writers to vocational training and many, many other things. Both programs, I think, were vital to the young people of those depression years to maintain their understanding of the work ethic. Today, we have so split up all our youth activities and diversified them into so many different departments. I think there are something like four hundred fifty-four different agencies of government now dealing with temporary employment and vocational training for young people. He would have been horrified by that splitting up of an essential function which is to keep the work ethic going in young people.

As I go around the country today I constantly run into doctors and lawyers and businessmen who say, "Mr. Roosevelt, I just want to tell you I got my start in the CCC." That was very significant. I wish that President Reagan could, in his admiration for FDR, consolidate the entire youth effort of government. I am not saying whether it ought to be state or city administered or federally administered, but we have all these programs and they should be brought together. I'll talk about the reorganization of government a little bit later.

He was also influenced, of course, by the La Follettes and people like Burt Wheeler who were the Progressives of that day. But fundamentally he was a pragmatist. If a program didn't work he would throw it out and be perfectly frank about it. Can you imagine Lyndon Johnson saying that part of his "great society" program didn't work? It would have been totally "un-Lyndon." But FDR was strong enough within himself to say, "That didn't work. We'll try something else." It is a very important characteristic of his presidency that distinguishes him from subsequent presidents.

He was also a pragmatist in the evolving civil rights movement of the thirties. I was here at law school and I remember going up and having dinner with him one night in the Oval Room upstairs in the White House, just on a card table, the two of us. I was quite horrified by the lynchings that were still going on in the South and I was accusing him of not being a leader on this issue. There was a bill in the Congress, an anti-lynching bill. Can you imagine that today? That's only forty-odd years ago. He said, "Franklin, I can't move too quickly. The president has not only to lead the country but also he is the chief trustee and guardian of the national security." This was in 1938, my first year in law school. And he said, "I can see a trend towards a new world war and I am going to need the votes of my southern Democrats in the Congress to prepare for that war. I cannot alienate them over the issue of civil rights. While civil rights is vital and I would like to do something, I would like to lead on that, but I would so alienate my southern Democrats in the Congress that I would not be able to carry forward the neccessary preparation for this country in case World War II comes."

Now you remember through 1938 and 1939 the Congress kept repeatedly turning down his requests to begin the rearmament of the navy and the army. The air force was part of the army in those days and the navy had their own air force and the marines had their own air force. But he was constantly held back by the Congress and yet he was able to get the draft through. If you remember, in September of 1941, three months before Pearl Harbor, he was able to get the draft extended by one vote in the House, one vote. That's how close we came to disbanding the draft three months before Pearl Harbor. He was able to do the Lend-Lease Deal, and the fifty destroyers to England in return for bases, without congressional approval which is the expansion of the presidency under Roosevelt. But, as we got closer and closer to World War II, he did have the support of his southern Democrats in the Congress. I think this is a perfect example of his pragmatism, putting civil rights on the back burner, keeping national security on the front burner. A very important example.

He was also a pramatist in getting things done. There was a vacancy on the circuit court of appeals in this circuit and Harry Byrd, Sr. wanted a very conservative good old hack politician from the Byrd organization to be named to this vacancy. My father didn't want any part of Harry Byrd's nomination. Well, as you know one of the Senate courtesy procedures provides that if the senator in question does not approve of a presidential nominee, it does not go through. My father was telling me of his difficulties with Harry Byrd in filling this judicial appointment one evening again, just alone over dinner on a card table. And I said, "Well, you know, you've got a perfect solution. There's a wonderful former dean of the University of Virginia Law School, Armistead Dobie, who happens to be one of the most respected experts on federal procedure. Now Harry Byrd certainly could not oppose the dean of his own law school." He said, "My gosh, you've got him." And the next day he called Armistead Dobie on the phone right then and there from the White House. You remember Dobie was very much of an extrovert. He had some problems but he had a wonderful, wonderful brilliant mind. They got along famously and very quickly—and very shortly in those days because I don't think they bothered with FBI investigations that take six to ten weeks—his name was sent up to the Senate and Harry Byrd was stopped. Again a very pragmatic approach to the day-to-day operation of government.

When he became president, FDR realized that economic policy was difficult to formulate because we had no real knowledge of what was happening in the economy. So, he started the Bureau of Labor Statistics, and now, of course, the Commerce Department. The Commerce Department and the Bureau of Labor Statistics and other agencies began doing a lot of research on the day-to-day trends within the economy. Therefore economic policy today is based much more on facts than it was when he came in in 1933. When FDR started the Bureau of Labor Statistics and named a remarkable man from New York, a professor of economics, Isador Lubin, as its head, he put together the beginnings of what is now the statistical information that the federal government has available to the president, to the Council of Economic Advisors, to the private sector and so forth. So I think, again, that was a very pragmatic recognition of a vacuum and it was solved quickly.

Let us go on quickly to the war years, which were an entirely separate phase of his presidency. The domestic policy really went on the back burner after Pearl Harbor. His relationship with Churchill, I think, was one of the great fortuitous relationships in the history of the world. These two men understood each other, as well as admired each other, and had a great personal liking for each other, although they had tremendous fights. They both recognized that each was acting in the best interest of his own country, and, in Churchill's case, the empire: "I was not made the King's chief minister to preside over the dissolution of the Empire." You remember that marvelous phrase. Churchill, on the other hand, recognized that Roosevelt was not only always going to act in the United States' best interest, but that Roosevelt had the power: "We were the arsenal of democracy," to use his words. So, Churchill considered himself a junior partner. Then there was a much lower echelon of junior partners such as DeGaulle and Giraud. Roosevelt really was the war leader. Stalin was off in another corner.

Again, I think my father was more pragmatic, although many people will still argue about Yalta. If my father had lived he would have held Stalin's feet to the fire, living up to the terms of the Yalta Agreement. Truman just didn't know enough about how the Yalta Agreement evolved, nor was he strong enough to stand up to Stalin and make him live up to the Yalta Agreement as it applied to Eastern Europe. And of course Churchill went out, was elected out. But, the relationship between Churchill and Roosevelt was, I think, epitomized by the fact that my father always called the

Prime Minister, "Winston," and Winston always called my father, "Mr. President." This was a very subtle but significant difference, if you will.

At some times the relationship also was one of needling each other, of being amused by each other. I will never forget the Four Freedoms meeting at Argentia Bay, Newfoundland in August of 1941. My destroyer was on the Atlantic patrol at the time and we were ordered into Argentia Bay and I was ordered over to his flagship, USS Augusta, to be my father's temporary junior naval aide. I had charge of the boat pool to get all the generals and admirals to the right meetings on the right cruisers. Churchill used to stand up after dinner and recite poetry, Shakespeare, Shelley, Keats, Wordsworth, you name it. He could just stand there and this marvelous rolling Churchillian memory would come forth. It was entertainment at its zenith. Of course, Churchill loved the center stage. In the conferences Churchill was always the junior partner but after dinner he became center stage.

At Casablanca, where my destroyer had brought in the first convoy in January, 1943, from the States, I went ashore for a couple of days during that meeting. At lunch the first day Giraud was there; my father had produced Giraud. The word from London was that DeGaulle wouldn't come, he was pouting. He didn't want to see Giraud and he didn't want to have any part of making any agreements with Giraud. So at lunch my father turned and said, "Winston, now I produced the groom, you produce the bride." And Churchill said, "But Mr. President, you know DeGaulle, you just can't tell him. You can't order him to come. He won't come." "Ah," my father said, "but you have the purse strings. Three days from now is payroll Friday, and the Free French will go without pay if DeGaulle doesn't come tomorrow." Winston said, "What a brilliant idea." Off went the telegram to London: "Tell General DeGaulle no payroll on Friday unless he's in Casablanca tomorrow." DeGaulle arrived! I think Churchill learned the pragmatic use of power from my father on that occasion!

He also, of course, inherited certain characteristics of his administration. Except for TR, he was really the first great conservationist president. He always had tremendous admiration for TR and Gifford Pinchot, both Republicans. Under FDR's presidency the whole national park system, the federal land system, grew at a fantastic pace; he wanted to preserve the great wilderness and the great natural resources of this country.

He gave enormous momentum to the Civil Service Commission because he did not believe in the spoil system of President Jackson, who was its great exemplar. He believed in a professional civil service but he never thought about how the civil service could become a sinecure for incompetence. I think that if he had lived he would have taken drastic steps to change the qualifications for continuation and promotion in Civil Service status. I think he would have used the Navy system of quarterly reports by your commanding officer, and they've got to be damn good; otherwise no promotion. Again, being a pragmatist he would have realized that his goal of professionalism in government service was being undermined by those who were incompentent and were looking upon it as a safe haven. I think he would have corrected that.

One other very important point. Today I hear so often people saying: "If only the country could make a national effort to solve the energy crisis as we did with the Manhattan project." I think there is a major difference. Remember that the Manhattan project was ultra, ultra secret. Only one or two members of the cabinet knew about it. The vice-president himself, Harry Truman, did not know about it. Stimson told him about it after FDR died. It was done purely by executive order and the Congress had no notion of it whatsoever. I think the leaders of both the House and the Senate were informed but only in very guarded ways.

I think that my father respected the constitutional procedures and the responsibilities of the Congress more than subsequent presidents. I refer to you his complete acceptance when the Supreme Court declared the AAA and the NRA unconstitutional. There was no question of executive overriding of the Supreme Court decision. He did then try what was commonly called the "packing plan" of the Supreme Court, but when Alben Barkley told him that that was no good he backed off. Then enough of the nine old men resigned and he was able to get his Court. But, he did not change it from nine to sixteen. He was a constitutionalist. I can't say that in every case and in every act of subsequent presidents. I don't think, for example, that Richard Nixon was really a devoted constitutionalist. I am saying this very objectively. I happen to personally like Richard Nixon very much.

So, I think that's very important. He was a pragmatist and a constitutionalist. He got his way in the end, but he did not override the Supreme Court. He did not force the Congress, even though he had an enormous majority, to put through his packing plan when his own Senate Majority Leader, Alben Barkley, told him no.

But, to get back to "energy" and the Manhattan Project. They are not comparable. In times of peace this country cannot make a massive national effort except as we did in the space program under Kennedy when he made his decision, which really was the result of the Russians putting a man into space, the Sputnik. We react and we can develop a massive national effort to counter a foreign advantage which we consider, either through pride or through fear of military adaptation, the superior advance by a foreign nation. We could approach a national consensus in a massive national effort if the Russians, for example, were to develop a new unlimited supply of fuel through the use of hydrogen. I don't think, today, that nuclear energy, while it will have some limited growth, will be used as a total replacement for either oil or coal, largely because nobody has yet figured out what to do with the waste. Now you can say: well, a national scientific effort could find the waste solution. The French solution of putting it in glass is not really an unlimited solution for all time. But, you could not get the total consensus even by solving the waste problem. There are too many other fears about nuclear energy, especially since Three Mile Island. There are too many other fears to achieve a national consensus. I am convinced that by either solar energy or other developments we could solve the energy problem and become totally independent of OPEC if we did have that. We could do it if the Russians beat us to the punch or if OPEC suddenly gets stupid and if Saudi Arabia loses control of OPEC and they start jacking the prices and threaten the industrialized West with bankruptcy. Those two are the possible eventualities which would bring a national consensus on energy. But, except in wartime we cannot ever achieve the kind of project as the Manhattan Project. In peacetime it would have been really inconceivable to have undertaken, in my opinion.

I think that one of the tragedies has been that his successors, both Democrat and Republican, got confused between the temporary emergency solutions and the permanent floor under the economy, those two sides of the Roosevelt philosophy. As a result, without really understanding it, we moved in a socialist trend, greatly stimulated by Lyndon Johnson. I don't think he was enough of an intellectual to understand. He'd been in the Senate long enough so that when he suddenly got the power of the presidency thrust into his hands he went wild. A terribly difficult man.

Jack Royer and I set up, under the Civil Rights Act of 1964, the Equal Employment Opportunity Commission. It was very interesting to set up a new bureaucracy in Washington. We had very definite limits on the size of that agency. Today, the personnel is thirteen or fourteen times what it was when we set it up in 1965. That's only fifteen years and it has grown thirteen times.

I don't think we're going to see a change in the presidential term, say to six years, and a limitation of one term. I don't think we're going to come to that. I have serious questions about it because I think a four-year term does give us the right to throw out an incompetent, such as Jimmy Carter, who was my personal friend. Flexibility is terribly important in democracy. The biggest problem with the presidency today is that we have no job description. We hire our presidents without any regard to their qualifications, purely and simply on their abilities and talents on the tube. We do not have the marvelous insurance system that the British have with the loyal opposition as a shadow cabinet which is constantly informed of the intricacies of foreign relations, military policy, and so forth and so on. Immediately following a British election it can step in totally informed. And of course their cabinet and the prime minister come up through years and years of experience in the House of Commons, and occasionally through service in the House of Lords, Lord Halifax, for example. We throw out our outgoing senior cabinet officers and subcabinet officers and they usually vanish from public service—very wasteful.

Now we've got a slight modification. We have the Brookings Institution and now this new one which the so-called right has formed, the American Enterprise Institute. We have these two havens for outgoing bureaucrats of appointed levels—they're not really bureaucrats. This is good because they do keep informed and you do see the same old faces coming back at the second and third echelons. When the Democrats come back the same old faces come back in again, and when the Republicans come in you see the same old faces among the Republicans, although there are fewer of them. But that's good. I'm all in favor of that, but I don't think that we should address ourselves to constitutional changes of time or repetition or reelection, either in the House or the Senate or the presidency. I think this system has worked well enough for over two hundred years and we ought to not scrap it or modify it without deep, deep thought. With the rapidity with which the events evolve today in the world the flexibility of our system must be our strength and we should not hamper that flexibility. I think that we should address ourselves to the question of job qualification.

Now I have no quick answers. I only suggest that perhaps serving as governor of a state like Georgia is different from serving as the governor of a state like California or New York. I am not sure that congressional service is also not very important because of your knowledge of how to get things done in Washington, which is an art in itself. My father understood that because he had served the eight years of the Wilson administration as undersecretary of the navy—it was then called assistant secretary of the navy. There was only one assistant secretary. And he learned then how to get things done in Washington, which stood him in good stead. He was also a member of the state legislature, so he understood the legislative process. Jimmy Carter, coming from Georgia, did not have these kinds of qualifications.

I think also one important quality of a president is his ability and willingness to pick able people and not be afraid of them. Jimmy Carter was scared to death of able people around him because he was insecure himself. Lyndon Johnson, to some extent, had that same fear. I saw it, discussed it with him. Reagan is remarkable. I don't say his cabinet is as good as I would have liked but I say that his White House staff is probably the best we have seen since the first presidential assistant, Jim Rowe, was appointed. When you look back at Woodrow Wilson's White House staff, it was minuscule. The committee system of General Motors has some interesting applications to the federal government. Reagan is beginning to apply this more than any other president—the committee system.

I think also of a new Hoover commission to realign the structure of the executive branch by function rather than by historical fiat, which is really what it is today. That's why so many functions are spread out all over the governmental structure. They shouldn't be. I mentioned earlier the youth programs. We should reorganize government on a functional basis. My father did approve of a Defense Department because he believed that all the military should be coordinated, in a technological era, in which the same plane can serve marines, navy and air force. It doesn't work too well for many reasons but that was his theory. I think that a functional reorganization of government, plus the job qualifications of the candidates for the presidency, are areas of real concern which this center should study.

Press conferences: I'm very pleased that Ronald Reagan followed the recommendations of this center in his press conferences, which was nothing but a circus under previous presidents. The personality of my father prevented his press conferences from becoming a circus. But basically, press conferences in today's world are where each word has enormous subtle implications. Let's just take the Middle East situation, the Arab-Israel situation. There is a whole vocabulary, as all of you know, of words which mean one thing to Israel and another thing to the Arabs. They both understand what each means by the use of the same word and they both understand the differences. But when a president in a press conference misuses a word, a technical word, it doesn't look technical. It may be spelled just the way you and I would spell it, but when a president, through a slip, misuses a word, that has tremendous diplomatic and perhaps even greater implications. That was done by Jerry Ford once or twice. Press conferences are very dangerous for presidents in this very volatile world. I personally believe that if you get a president like FDR or like Jack Kennedy who was enormously intelligent and bright then a press conference is safe.

I am not sure that unless Ronald Reagan has his file cards the press conference is safe for him to be exposed to questions. Now that's not a criticism, I respect Ronald Reagan for using his card system on issues. I think that is an example of playing it safe. But, a press conference is a very dangerous thing. Jimmy Carter's became a total circus. So, I think press conferences depend on the intelligence and the ability of the president involved, basically because they are so dangerous in this world of instant communications and very, very technical meanings to words in the diplomatic jargon. I would almost recommend that questions should be written and answers prepared ahead of time. Now this doesn't mean that you can't use television and so forth, but the format has got to set up safeguards now, and I think your recommendations of changing the format is a very strong step in the right direction. But I would go even further.

I know that I have talked too long on the growth of the presidency, but I see a swing back. I think one of the first steps is Congress trying to regain some of its authority which has been slowly eroded by strong presidents. For example, the limitations on the executive getting us into wars following the Vietnam situation. I think the restoration of the balance is good as long as it does not interfere with the flexibility and the quickness of decision making, because events happen so quickly and communication is so instant that the president has to be able to react instantly.

So, with apologies for too many words, I want to thank you very much for inviting me. I suppose now we can have some questions from the experts, which I am not.

NARRATOR: We have two scholar/panelists who will raise particular questions, but we also have all kinds of assorted scholars and observers and participants around the table. So maybe the best way to proceed would be for Mr. Shannon to ask a couple of questions and Mr. Graebner will follow with a few more, and then open it up to general discussion.

MR. SHANNON: My first question is a broad one and then I have a more specific question which arose from Tom Corcoran's visit here earlier. Of what domestic legislation was he the proudest?

MR. ROOSEVELT: I think, really, unemployment insurance and ultimately social security. I think they met the two standards that I set. They protected the individual from those circumstances over which he had no control, but they also were setting the floor under the economy which he considered to be of great importance, maintaining a minimum national purchasing power. Of course, the purchasing power evaporated in 1929 to 1932, and it was very slow coming back. I think I would pick out those two for his domestic program.

Now I think that Lend-Lease and the draft as preparation for war measures were the two programs in foreign policy. He really looked upon the "destroyers for bases" deal as a pretty good deal for the U.S. because here we had these World War I destroyers and he was delighted to get rid of them. The English did need something and Churchill was very pleased to get them. But, I would say the Lend-Lease and the extension of the draft; not really the first passage of the draft, but the extension of the draft. He actually called Congressman Klein, who had just been elected in the special election in Brooklyn and asked him to come down for his first vote to vote for the extension of the draft. That was the one vote by which he carried the extention of the draft in September, I think it was, in 1941. So, those two would be the wartime measures and social security and unemployment insurance would be the others.

MR. SHANNON: Tommy Corcoran said that your father and people quite close to him were not at all disappointed with the court case declaring NRA unconstitutional. I felt gratified to hear that because I figured that it got him off a bad hook, that NRA didn't work. It was one of those few, maybe the first case, on at least the federal level, of sunset legislation. It was enacted in June 1933, I guess, I'm not sure, and it was to expire June 30, 1935. There developed a lot of opposition within organized labor and particularly within small business. The administration bill introduced in 1935 fell for what was popularly called the skeletonized NRA and it wasn't getting anywhere. Then near the end of May it was struck down.

MR. ROOSEVELT: I agree with you. There's one other factor which confirms your belief, and Tommy's belief, and my belief. If you remember, after the NRA was passed there were quite a lot of people who were beginning to compare it to Mussolini's corporate state concept which resulted in fixed prices and was really quite contrary to my father's fundamental faith in competition, the work ethic, competition, and so forth. I think that my father was beginning to get very irritated with it being compared to the economic philosophy of Mussolini, whom he absolutely despised. He looked down upon him. He thought he was a pompous upstart. Roosevelt obviously could not have sat and enjoyed an evening with Mussolini as he did with Churchill. That's the best way to summarize it. In fact, he mentioned to me that he was very irritated by those people who were comparing his economic philosophy to Mussolini's.

Now the AAA was something else. There, I think, they made a concentrated effort to meet the Supreme Court's objections and to pass what they really looked at as setting a floor under the farm economy. The original concept has been broadened considerably depending on the status of the agricultural economy, such as the set aside of lands program which has now been dropped. There were all kinds of modifications that have come and gone in the farm bills that have followed. But with the AAA they firmly believed something should be done, because in 1933, on March 4th, corn was selling for five cents a bushel and wheat was selling for six cents a bushel. That was the degree to which the farmer was going bankrupt. Of course, the extension of the mortgages and all that were again emergency programs. They were not permanent programs. So I agree with you on NRA, but I point out the Mussolini implication. But that did not apply to the AAA.

MR. SHANNON: The next question has to do with your father's personal reaction to criticism. Perhaps Nixon is a recent case, but with your father it had been a very long time since any president had been a target for such severe attacks and often from very highly respected American citizens. Did this get to him, did it bother him?

MR. ROOSEVELT: He had the hide of an elephant. He had the ability to go to sleep at night and sleep like a baby. I think basically he was such a smart politician that he decided where the votes were, and the votes weren't on Wall Street. The votes weren't in the public utility executive group. The votes weren't in the automobile industry executive suites. They were with the union guys. You remember the sitdown strikes. You remember Governor Murphy, who later went on the Supreme Court. I think he was, again, being totally pragmatic. He went where the votes were. Here he was the champion of the forgotten man. But he curried the opposition even though he made attacks in campaigns and in between campaigns on the great power of the great corporations and their selfishness and their ruthlessness. Having cultivated that opposition he was very divisive. There's no question about it. He played divisive politics, but he played it with an overwhelming majority of the votes that was his. Having made that decision it didn't bother him at all what the Liberty League and the DuPonts and all the rest called him. He expected that they would fight, and he would have wondered why they didn't fight back because he was a fighter and he respected people who fought. So, it wasn't just a tough elephant hide; it was a carefully thought out pragmatic approach to the politics of that day.

I don't agree with those that say you can't draw certain lessons today. Obviously, the specifics of the Roosevelt era program would not necessarily apply today, but I think that we do learn lessons from the past. Ronald Reagan is showing an ability to build a popular majority. He hasn't really consolidated it yet but it's beginning. For example, I don't know if Ronald Reagan has thought of this, but I think today we are on the threshold of an entirely new labor/management or worker/management relationship. I really prefer today to use the word "worker" rather than labor because of connotations of union labor, organized labor and so on. Industry is becoming, through technology, so highly skilled—the whole robot system, the whole computerization of what happens as the car goes down the line—that the worker who has any drive or ambition goes to school at night to learn a new skill to learn how to operate all the new high technology machinery. We're going to develop a class of highly skilled, highly trained workers. What concerns me is that there will be a third element in the worker group which we have not yet found a way of motivating, probably because they are difficult to train from their own inabilities and probably because they have no motivation. We could be approaching a situation of social structure where we have management, highly skilled workers, and then a pool of far less skilled who are going to find great difficulties in finding productive employment with an advancement future.

I think this country is beginning to move into this new era, but I don't know how fast it is going to happen. Bob Royer tells me that some of the steel companies are considering buying some of the new technology used in the Japanese steel industry. Certainly the automobile companies are. We are now robotizing welding, not only in the European companies, the Japanese companies, but in the Detroit companies. We eliminate rattles today from the car. That's the whole robotizing of the production line. So, we're on the verge of some very new developments. What that does to big labor, organized labor, it's too early really to think through.

If we move another step in copying the Japanese on their—I've forgotten what they call it—but it's making the worker group into part of management, giving suggestions about how to improve the product, how to improve the production line. They hold meetings and they're really part of the company family. If we get to that stage in labor relations, the National Labor Relations Act is going to have to go through a very major reorganization because the structure of union versus management is going to break down. It's going to be a new concept. Already in Germany we see labor members on the board of directors in the big companies. That's a horrifying thought for most of American industrial management, but I'll guarantee it will have arrived within ten years. Of course, Douglas Fraser is now on the board of Chrysler so that's the beginning, that's the opening wedge.

So, I think we're going to see that. But, not as something to fear because I think we're going to copy the Japanese, develop an Americanized concept of making the worker, not labor, a part of the corporate family. That's a new trend.

I do think we can learn from the philosophical approach of the past, and one of the things I have tried to emphasize today is the pragmatism of Roosevelt which recognizes the inevitability and necessity of change.

MR. GRAEBNER: I am going to turn to the question of foreign affairs. Throughout the 1930s the United States was potentially the most powerful nation in the world, and yet it had almost no influence on the policies of Germany and Japan that led to global war. Even the decision that eventually brought the United States into the main currents of world affairs was made in Tokyo and not in Washington. For this absence of genuine national policy, at least before September of 1939, there are two basic explanations. Some insisted President Roosevelt knew what the country needed but was prevented by an isolationist opinion. Others would insist that FDR and his advisors had little basic understanding of world affairs and thus were never able to transcend the utopian policies which they inherited from the Republican years. Now which of these two notions seems to be the more accurate to you?

MR. ROOSEVELT: I think the first. I think FDR had a good hunch—he used that word from time to time—of the trend toward World War II. I mentioned it in connection with why he put civil rights on a back burner. I remind you that he tried to rearm Guam and he couldn't get it through the Congress. I remind you of Lindbergh's visit to Germany, his subsequent meeting with Ambassador Kennedy in London, Lindbergh returning to a hero's welcome, not for flying the ocean but from the isolationist wing of American public opinion, and the firing of Kennedy as a result of his sympathy with the Lindbergh assessment of the German air force. I think my father was way ahead, but again, he had to trim his sails. Don't forget in that 1940 election: "I will never send an American to die on foreign soil." My God, you can say that that was the most hypocritical statement he ever made and perhaps it was. He must have known that that was not going to be a promise that he could keep.

But today, we see Ronald Reagan trying to modify social security, having promised in the campaign that there would be not cutbacks in the social security program. So I think a president is forced under our system to do certain things to get reelected. I think TR first said this, "First you've got to get elected before you can do anything good." And that is the prime rule of politics, get in there and then you can do something. So I would say that really Roosevelt and Sumner Welles were highly intelligent and highly farsighted in their understanding of the world situation. But because of its isolationist reluctance, Congress turned down all of his recommendations and stopped the buildup of the navy and the army appropriations. They turned him down flat. They, I think, approved the construction of one group of new destroyers prior to 1939.

So, I think that Welles was very important in this, much more so than Cordell Hull, partly because FDR and Welles had better communications, but they also understood the world situation. Still, they were enormously hampered by the Congress and the isolationist feeling in this country. Again, I simply point to the one vote in September for the continuation of the draft. The isolationists in Congress and throughout the country did not want to even think about being part of World War II.

MR. GRAEBNER: I would like to just pose one other question as a followup. Your father had such a remarkable capacity to communicate. He did so, effectively, on all matters of domestic affairs, particularly his fireside chats which were certainly remarkable.

Now if he had the convictions about foreign affairs that you suggest then I'm wondering why he never embarked on any similar effort to communicate to the American people the realities of world affairs and to achieve some kind of success that would be comparable to what he did actually achieve on matters of the American economy.

MR. ROOSEVELT: You're absolutely right, he did not. And the proof of this is his remark in the 1940 election that no American boy would go overseas and die on foreign soil. Again, being the pragmatic politician that he was, I think he understood that the public opinion was overwhelmingly isolationist. The Congress was overwhelmingly isolationist. Now, he also believed that a leader could get just so far in front of the troops. If he got too far ahead he would be isolated and the troops would try to run the other way and he would be left there to be destroyed. Being a politician who did not enjoy losing and being destroyed, he felt that he just couldn't educate the American people, even knowing his ability through the fireside chats and press conferences. It was just too much for him to take on. In this case, I think that he felt that the events themselves had to generate the change from isolationism. You know, when you look at what he did achieve before Pearl Harbor to get this country ready, with the destroyers for bases deal, with the draft, he was moving as fast as he thought prudently he could go without being chopped off. I think that is the only answer to that question.

Now an idealist would say, "Well, he knew what the Japs and the Germans and the Italians were planning and he should have sacrificed himself to educate and lead the American people." But, he probably would have lost and we would have had Tom Dewey or Wendell Wilkie in 1940. And, I suppose an incumbent president always thinks that his opposition has none of his qualities of leadership!

QUESTION: It is true, isn't it, that your father, in 1937, made his famous speech on quarantining the aggressors, and the reaction to that was such that he could not have done much at all? Isn't that an indication of his attempt to do something here?

MR. ROOSEVELT: Yes and he found himself out on a limb.

QUESTION: This was the era of the Neutrality Act.

MR. ROOSEVELT: Yes, I had forgotten that. That's a very good example. He was on much safer ground with the Good Neighbor Policy. The American people understood our relationship to Latin America, to South America. But to Europe they were very, very skeptical. Remember, this is a country that had gotten away from all the problems of Europe and they did not want to be enmeshed in those problems. This is part of the psychological history of the isolationist's concept of America, which was very strong in the twenties and thirties following World War I. Remember, we turned down the League of Nations, overwhelmingly. My father ran for the vice-presidency with Cox in 1920 and they supported the League of Nations. There he stood, and he was the general, or lieutenant general, who got out in front of the troops and the limb was sawed off. And of all people, by Harding. I think the Democrats carried only six or eight states in the 1920 election. That was a big lesson for him. He was never going to get out on that damn limb again by himself. The troops were always going to be pretty damn close behind.

QUESTION: You suggested earlier that had FDR lived the Russians might not—at least this was the inference I drew—have taken over Eastern Germany, Poland and East Europe. I remember very vividly the situation at the end of the war. We'd been over there for three years. Half were shouting in a demagogic way, "Get us home immediately," and we were agreeing with them, of course. I just find it inconceivable that, short of dropping another atomic bomb on Moscow, anything could have been done that would have altered that situation.

MR. ROOSEVELT: Well, let me put it this way. We're talking "iffy" history. Remember that one of the last telegrams he sent, at Averell Harriman's insistence, was a telegram to Stalin reminding him of his commitment to free elections in Poland. I think that if he had lived—this is my personal opinion—he would have first mobilized—and he was very good at this—world public opinion, not American, but world public opinion to see that the Russians were reneging, that Stalin was reneging on the deal. I can just hear the rhetoric coming from him and Churchill: the right to self determination of the Eastern Europeans through free elections. Remember that the United Nations was just coming into being that June or July, following his death on April 12. This might have given the United Nations a whole "raison d'etre." It might have broken up that United Nations because the Russians might have pulled out, but it would have mobilized the noncommunist world to a degree. Remember, we still had Chiang Kai-shek running China, which was potentially a threat to the big border of Russia in the east. Plus, we had the atom bomb and they didn't. And the Third World countries were beginning to emerge and they would have supported self-determination in Eastern Europe.

Now that's very significant. Nobody has ever asked: would Roosevelt have ever dropped or threatened to drop another bomb?

I don't know. We're talking "iffy" politics. He was a master of using all the powers of the office in a very pragmatic way. I can conceive of his threatening to use the atom bomb against the Russians. I can conceive of a summit meeting with Chiang Kai-shek in which Chiang Kai-shek would have threatened the eastern borders of Russia. And remember, the Russians were pretty tired of war, too. So, now whether they would have actually implemented those threats, nobody can tell. But, I certainly think that he would have put up a hell of a bigger and stronger fight than Truman did, largely because Truman came into something where he didn't even know what was going on.

We're talking "iffy" history, but I think he would have mobilized world opinion, he would have used threats, he would have had a fast meeting with Chiang Kaishek, and Russia would have been suddenly very, very surrounded. It was later followed by John Foster Dulles in his regional groupings that surrounded and contained the Russians' expansionist policy, which for a short time was quite effective.

I know as an historian you tend to downgrade those possibilities but I simply say they are strong possibilities. Whether they go as far as being probabilities or not, I don't know.

DUMAS MALONE: I was living in Washington at the time of the transition from the Hoover to the Roosevelt administration and it was by all odds the most exciting period in my entire life. I heard your father's inaugural address. About six weeks after that I wrote a little article, very obscure, I'm sure nobody here has ever read it, which I entitled "Jefferson and the New Deal." It was published in *Scribner's* magazine. It announced the idea that he was pursuing Jeffersonian ends with Hamiltonian means. Of course, that's a great oversimplification, but he was quite prepared to use power, of which Jefferson was extremely fearful, and he was very pragmatic as of course Jefferson was. But, the Jeffersonian ends I was thinking of—foreign affairs was not in it at that time, it was domestic—were human interest and human values. He was struggling with a fearful economic situation. Of course, economic considerations and human considerations overlapped. They're inseparable, in fact, but they are not identical. I have the feeling, and always had it, that your mother may have been considerably responsible for this, but it was not merely a matter of calculation. He did put human values first, did he not?

MR. ROOSEVELT: I tried to say that, in my opinion, he was balancing the economic side with the human misery side and I said that I thought that social security and unemployment insurance were probably the two domestic achievements of which he was most proud. I can't tell you whether it's the economic or the human side which was most important in those two pieces of legislation. It was a combination. I don't know which was preeminent.

In my mother's mind, the human side, the social side, was the most important. She really was not interested in economics. But, he realized the importance of economics and when he could play the two together for both economic and human reasons then he was very satisfied.

One final point, I think your analysis of Jefferson's objectives using Hamiltonian methods is very accurate, even though it's an oversimplification. But I think that actually Hamilton was much more of a theorist. He believed in the importance of a strong central government. Jefferson believed in states' rights. In that era there was a massive argument, as we all know, throughout the country about states' rights and federal power, centralized authority, if you want. That was no longer really an important issue in 1933. The nation faced the disaster of the depression and there was no question that the federal government was going to have to move, that the states were no longer able to resolve their unemployment and depression problems. So, the philosophical argument of the Jefferson-Hamiltonian days was not even an argument in 1933. It was resolved by the circumstances. And we have seen the results.

Now, of course, Reagan is trying to return to the states, not the philosophy of a program, but the adminsitration of a program. Again, it's very significant. What Reagan is doing—I don't think most people realize it—but we're going through a real revolution of curtailing the federal government power, particularly in the administrative end. It's a much more significant revolution which is going on today in Washington than most people realize.

NARRATOR: Maybe the best way to thank you is to say that if Jack Royer had any doubts about why you got the degree when you did from law school, we don't have any now.

MR. ROOSEVELT: May I make one comment on that. My father was elected an honorary member of Phi Beta Kappa and wore his Phi Beta key in a bit of a phoney way in his lapel, very proudly even though he was only an honorary member. To my knowledge, and I've searched the family history, my daughter, Laura, is the first legitimate Phi Beta Kappa in the Roosevelt family. I might add she got all the talent from her mother.

FDR AND THE PRESIDENTIAL PRESS CONFERENCE

Chalmers M. Roberts

NARRATOR: I welcome you to a Miller Center Forum. To prepare you for the profession which Mr. Chalmers Roberts represents, one of our colleagues went to the library and read the following quotation from Walter Winchell: "A columnist is someone who finds out things that people do not know and tells them to people to whom it doesn't make any difference." It apparently has made considerable difference over the years to many people that Chalmers Roberts was at his place and at his station, following the events of the nation and of its leaders. I met three working journalists the other day and we began comparing notes about writers and they made the comment that it was in the days of Alfred Friendly, Carroll Kilpatrick, and Chalmers Roberts, the early days — in the forties and fifties — that the *Washington Post* reached its greatest heights. That was the day, they said, when people worked ever harder at uncovering facts and discovering what lay behind some of the events that flashed by. That reputation, I think, undoubtedly began early for Chalmers Roberts. He both ended and began with the *Post.* In 1933 and 1934 he was with the *Post,* then the *Toledo News Bee,* then the *Japanese Times* in Tokyo, the *Washington Daily News, Washington Times Herald,* on the staff of *OWI, Life* magazine, the *Washington Star,* but then in 1949 returned to the *Washington Post.* He covered local and national news beats in the beginning, became chief diplomatic correspondent, then a contributing columnist. He received awards from the Washington Newspaper Guild for national news reporting, from the Overseas Press Club, and the Washington Newspaper Guild Front Page Grand Prize Award, the Raymond Clapper Memorial

Award, the Edward Weintal Prize for Diplomatic Reporting, and the Frank Luther Mott Research Award. He is the author of *Washington Past and Present, Can We Meet the Russians Half Way?, The Nuclear Years: The Arms Race and Arms Control 1945-70, First Rough Draft: A Journalist's Journal of Our Times,* and then the much discussed history of *The Washington Post: The First 100 Years,* one of the few extended histories and reviews of any newspaper.

For those who struggle with their writing and sometimes see fewer results than one would like, they can be consoled and reassured that even with both members of the Roberts family struggling and striving to write and to edit, the book took four years in preparation. I remember an earlier incarnation of Chalmers Robrts around a conference table in New York. One of the memories that has stuck with me was here was a newspaper man who not only had a point of view but who was willing to listen in a discussion group. So, it is a great pleasure to have him with us.

This is the fourth in a series on the Roosevelt presidency. Maybe the Roosevelt presidency and the Roosevelt Press Conference will be only a point of departure—that remains to be seen, but it is a pleasure that we can both listen and ask questions of one of America's most respected columnists, Chalmers Roberts.

MR. ROBERTS: Thank you. I have to say first that that extended biography of the places I have worked reminds me that I once went someplace to get a job and the managing editor said to me, "Where have you worked?" I rattled off all these places thinking, "Good experience; I looked good." And he said, "You're just a drifter, aren't you?"

On Tuesday, May 18, 1937, President Roosevelt began his 367th press conference by saying, "I am going to ask you for a very few minutes to resolve ourselves into a Committee of the Whole. Off the record, wholly off the record. I wanted to tell you a story that I think you ought to know because it does affect the press of the country. I think you will all agree on that, when you hear what I am going to read. As you know, I have always encouraged, and am entirely in favor of, absolute freedom for all news writers. That should be and will continue to be the general rule in Washington."

What FDR went on to say was this: The McClure Syndicate circulated to some 270 newspapers each week a pink sheet containing information for editors, a sort of confidential news tip sheet. This was in addition to so-called white sheets, stories intended for publication. The president then read from the latest pink sheet, to wit:

> Unchecked. A New York specialist high in the medical field is authority for the following, which is given in the strictist con-

fidence to editors: "Toward the end of last month Mr. Roosevelt was found in a coma at his desk. Medical examination disclosed the neck rash which is typical of certain disturbing symptoms. Immediate treatment of the most skilled kind was indicated, with complete privacy and detachment from official duties. Hence the trip to southern waters, with no newspapermen on board and a naval convoy which cannot be penetrated."

The unusual activities of Vice President Garner are believed to be in connection with the current situation and its possible developments. "Checking has been impossible."

Roosevelt then read a second item, also from the syndicate. It concerned a private dinner in New York at which an official of American Cyanamid had called the president "the paranoiac in the White House," and had gone on to declare that, "a couple of well placed bullets would be the best thing for the country, and that he for one would buy a bottle of champagne as quick as he could get it to celebrate such news."

There followed some give and take between FDR and the reporters during which the president said that the editor of the offending syndicate was one Richard Waldo. At one point a reporter asked: "Isn't that second one—(the second item)—actionable under law?"

To which FDR replied: "You know, that does not make any difference at all. The President of the United States does not sue for libel and the Department of Justice does not proceed for libel."

After taking up about half the press conference time, that is, about fifteen minutes I would estimate, FDR reiterated that, "It is all off the record; all strictly in the family and nothing else." And finally he said, "The Committee (of the Whole) will now recess." Whereupon the president went on to talk about and take questions on the topical issues of the day.

To the best of my knowledge all of the two hundred or so reporters—and they included a few, very few, women—observed FDR's off-the-record rule. Nothing appeared in the public prints or on radio newscasts. This was pre-television, of course. Everybody in town naturally soon heard all about it by word of mouth. Some indignant members of the press struck at Richard Waldo, the offending editor, by having the National Press Club's board of governors call on him to show cause why he should not be expelled for insulting a fellow member—FDR. Waldo appeared—and here I quote from Oliver Clapper's 1946 book—"and threatened each board member with libel action, declaring that their homes, savings, et cetera, would be seized if he won. The board members naturally hesitated. No formal action ever was taken but Mr. Waldo nevertheless went out of the club." I assume he resigned.

I have cited this incident in some detail because I think it tells us a great deal, in retrospect, about the relationship between FDR and the press.

My premise today is that FDR was the best presidential communicator—to use the current term—in modern times. His honeymoon with the press lasted about two years, an extraordinary length of time. But the honeymoon did end and the normal press-president adversary relationship came into play. The approach of World War II sharpened antagonisms prior to Pearl Harbor; afterwards, both a sense of patriotism and military censorship widened the gap between press and president until his death.

In reflecting on FDR and the press, I think it is vital to go back to the beginning of his first term. I did not come to Washington until October 1933, seven months after his inauguration, but the mood I describe here was instantly evident to even a cub reporter just out of college earning fifteen dollars a week on the *Washington Post*.

You must remember that by 1933, as historian John Morton Blum has put it, "the presidency had lost the stature that Theodore Roosevelt and Wilson had given it." In the Harding-Coolidge era of the 1920s New York, not Washington, dominated the nation. The Great Depression brought demands for federal action, largely resisted by President Hoover. By the end of Hoover's term, and the depth of the Depression, relations between president and press were absymal, just about non-existent. So when FDR moved down from Albany his opportunity to change that relationship, and to do so to his advantage, was immense—and he seized that opportunity. '

At his first press conference a few days after his inauguration each of the two hundred or so who crowded into the Oval Office was introduced to the president who shook hands. Some he recognized from Albany or the campaign and he called them by their first names. You must remember that he was seated behind his desk which made it difficult for those in the back to hear, and just about impossible to see him. I know because at times I stood in the back rows, in 1933–34.

That first day FDR announced that he would divide what he wanted to say into (1) statements attributable to him but only in indirect quotation, (2) material for direct quotation which was relatively rare and usually on request of reporters to use, in quotes, some striking phrase, (3) background information that showed up in print under such euphemisms as "the president is known to think that . . ." and (4) off the record information ranging from the incident I have cited to comments on individuals or nations that often subtly colored the reporting about both.

All of this was such a switch from Hoover that at the end of that first press conference the reporters broke into applause. I don't believe that has ever happened again.

Why did they applaud? Because the reporters knew they were going to have access to news, the meat and potatoes of their profession. And because, as it turned out, that access was extensive and continuous. Despite the war FDR, in just over twelve years in the White House, held 998 press conferences, a sea change from his predecessors and a record unmatched by his successors. They usually were held on Tuesday mornings and Friday afternoons, to give a time break to afternoon and then morning papers. As Frank Luther Mott, dean of historians of journalism, put it, "He knew what newspapermen recognized as a good story, and he knew as well as they did how and when to 'break' it. Moreover, he was genial to the point of exuberance, and it was clear that he thoroughly enjoyed the give and take of the mass press conference." And of course FDR had a facility of phrases: the "horse and buggy" Supreme Court of the Nine Old Men, the "garden hose" to help the allies like helping a neighbor, the shift from "Dr. New Deal" to "Dr. Win the War."

The White House was much more open to the press in those years, especially the pre-war years. In some previous administrations the press, or some of them, had been invited to one or another of the rather formal annual White House receptions along with the top bureaucrats, the military and/or the diplomats. FDR gave the press its own annual reception. I remember them well. He sat in a chair in the East Room smiling up at us as we came up to shake hands. Eleanor was at his side. There was punch and snacks and dancing in both the East Room and outside on the top of the adjoining portico to the east wing. I relish a story about George Bookman, one of the *Post's* White House reporters. He and his date were still enjoying one such party at two o'clock in the morning when Mrs. Roosevelt said sweetly: "Isn't it a little late for ice cream?"

FDR's sense of humor was a winner with the press. One day, when he was laid up in bed with a cold, the *Post* pulled a classic typographical error. The page one headline read: FDR IN BED WITH COED. Hardly had that early edition reached the White House than a *Post* reporter picked up the phone to hear: "This is Frank Roosevelt. I'd like 100 copies of that first edition of the *Post*. I want to send it to all my friends." Alas, the circulation department had scurried out to recover all the papers from the corner stands and destroy them. FDR never got his 100 copies.

Roosevelt, as that veteran reporter Richard L. Strout recently put it in an interview, had charm and magnetism and an ability to think quickly. John Gunther wrote that in twenty minutes FDR's features "expressed amazement, curiosity, mock alarm, genuine interest, worry, rhetorical playing for suspense, sympathy, decision, playfulness, dignity, and surpassing charm." He knew how to answer and how to dodge. He knew how to play on particular egos and how to tell the reporters it was not they, he was sure, but their

Tory bosses, the publishers, who wrote such terrible things about him and his New Deal.

But the honeymoon could not last. After all, the issues are what count with reporters. When the New Deal began to run out of steam and when FDR took on the Supreme Court, some reporters grew critical, others outright hostile. Occasionally FDR would tell a particular reporter to go stand in the corner with a dunce cap for asking what he considered a silly or dumb question, but that seemed mostly to be in jest. With the coming of the bitter pre-war struggle over possible American participation in World War II some press relationships grew extremely hostile and some of this continued after Pearl Harbor. At one point FDR awarded a hypothetical iron cross to a reporter. It happened this way. John O'Donnell, who wrote for the *New York News* which had been bitterly isolationist, reported that the army was issuing contraceptives to the WACs, the new woman's army corps. He had gotten the story, I'm told, from Clare Luce who was no FDR admirer. Roosevelt knew it was true but he took the tack that to say so in print was unpatriotic. O'Donnell, himself, avoided Roosevelt press conferences so at the next one FDR asked Earl Godwin, one of the front row regulars known as a Roosevelt fan, to give the iron cross to O'Donnell. Whether a medal actually was handed to Godwin, let alone O'Donnell, I don't know—I doubt it—but the incident left a sense of bitterness against the president even among journalists who thought little of O'Donnell himself. It certainly was one of FDR's least admirable moments.

That Roosevelt had reason to dislike—yes, hate—some of the barons of the press in that pre-TV era is evident from another incident. In 1935, as the honeymoon was ending, he got hold of an international Hearst empire message from a Hearst executive to its news service, saying "The Chief (as William Randolph Hearst liked to be called) instructs that the phrase Soak the Successful be used in all references to the administration's tax program instead of the phrase Soak the Thrifty hitherto used; also he wants the words Raw Deal used instead of New Deal." James MacGregor Burns recounted that an indignant FDR wanted to make the message public but that more prudent counsel prevailed. Anti-Roosevelt publishers used to complain that FDR had hypnotized their Washington reporters with his charm and misled them with his propaganda, as Leo Rosten put it in his 1937 book on *The Washington Correspondents.*

One of the reporters who had come down from Albany with Roosevelt was Ernest K. Lindley who had written the first FDR biography. But when Lindley wrote something FDR disliked about a New York political fight, the president demanded, at a press conference, that the reporter apologize. On another occasion he denied a Lindley story that FDR had picked Secretary of State Hull to be his successor in 1940 and that he had vetoed Jim Farley because he was a Catholic. At the next press conference Roosevelt said the story was made of whole cloth but that, as the *Post* next day put it in paraphrase, he considered Lindley's to be, "one of the most respected columns that he considered only about twenty percent wrong, as against other columns that are eighty percent wrong." Incidentally, reporters then had no access to the White House transcript of press conferences and the tape recorder was not yet born.

When the president is an activist the press tends to play him up as an individual. Witness Kennedy and now Reagan. In FDR's case, as Reston put it in 1937, "The Washington correspondents had propagated the impression that Franklin D. Roosevelt was a paragon of talents and a repository of supreme political skills. Events which shattered this idea released that iconoclasm which is the successor to faith." Something akin to that has been happening in Washington this fall.

It is always easier for historians, especially in such a lovely setting as we are in today, to look back, read the now available printed record, reflect and then discern the strands of greatness or of failure in any presidency. Roosevelt's unprecedented twelve years in the White House centered on two of the most cataclysmic events of our national existence, the Great Depression and World War II. And we still argue about the economics of the former and the causes of the latter.

The press in those great events was a conveyor belt between government and public. The correspondents who crowded into those 998 press conferences were the technicians for that process. On occasion individual journalists did influence the course of history or deflect government from its course. But even such occasions were incidental to the conveyor belt function. Then, as now, the messenger—to change the metaphor—often brought unpleasant news and the recipients of the news, the public, cried out for the head of the messenger. Remember Watergate.

What was the lasting role, the historical role, of the press in the age of Roosevelt? Did it go beyond the role of the messenger, the function of the conveyor belt that applies to all administrations?

Yes, it did, and it did so just as FDR's four administrations have affected our nation for almost a half century since that first inauguration day. In time, many of the New Deal measures have been altered, watered down, strengthened, or otherwise changed. But the central point—that the federal government has basic obligations to its citizenry—remains, though it clearly has been, and today still is, under challenge. Nonetheless, I do not think we are going to see a return to the states' rights, or to the county poorhouses, of pre-FDR eras.

Those of us in the press who came of age in the FDR years could no more escape being influenced by him and his New Deal and his internationalism than could the nation as a whole. And the influence has been just as lasting. I believe that only the influence on the press of the American Revolution and of the Civil War have matched that of FDR and of his stewardship of the New Deal and his direction of the allied effort in World War II. More than one generation of newsmen and women in Washington—and indeed all across the land—have reflected that, myself included. Many were isolationists in foreign affairs and believers in states' rights, or at least in state responsibility, in domestic affairs. It is true, as conservatives have been contending for some time now, that the press, most especially the Washington press, tends to be liberal in its outlook, probably more so than the public as a whole. And that is true not only of those remaining few of us who were here in Washington with FDR in 1933 but of most of those who arrived prior to Pearl Harbor. Those who came to the capital in, say, 1939, right out of college, are today the most senior among the current crop of active journalists. Nor should we neglect the effect on a second generation of journalists who were in grade school, or not even born, during the Depression and who now can vividly recall their parents' accounts of FDR and the New Deal, just as the oldest among us still can recall tales of the venerable Civil War veterans of our own early years.

It is worth mentioning, too, that the FDR aura is still remembered by our political leaders, notably by Ronald Reagan. His obeisance to the New Deal he remembers from his youth is evident in what he calls the social "safety net." That net may be getting ragged nowadays but before FDR there was no net at all, as Reagan well remembers. Perhaps Lyndon Johnson's Great Society today is being dismantled in large degree, but FDR's New Deal at home and his internationalism abroad remains very much central to this nation and journalists by and large reflect this.

Today it is hard to imagine a Washington press corps all crowded into the rather small Oval Office. It is hard to imagine a president who never appeared on television and for whom the radio was a rather sparingly used device to go over the heads of the antagonistic press lords to the voters. And for whom the twice weekly press conference thus was so vital a means of communication and influence. But all that was true of FDR and even to recall it is, to me, both a stimulating exercise and a refreshing reminder that this nation, the press very much included, is far better off today for Franklin D. Roosevelt having passed this way. Thank you.

QUESTION: You mentioned two hundred people going into the Oval Room for the Rooseveltian press conferences. Did that number increase during the twelve years he served or did it remain constant?

MR. ROBERTS: Well, there was a physical space limitation in the White House. To my knowledge, I don't know that anybody ever really counted how many went in. We used to line up in the hallway outside. This was true in Truman's administration too, until the White House was torn apart and he had to move across the street to the Blair House. Then he used the Executive Office Building which then Eisenhower used. We really never got back in the Oval Office. By then, there were too many people. We used to stand outside and Steve Early, who was Roosevelt's press secretary, would stand there and let us in past, I guess, one or two Secret Service types. Everybody had a press card that had been issued by the Secret Service and we filed in. The press associations and the regulars representing the major papers and the radio stood around Roosevelt's desk in the front, and the rest of us jockeyed to get in the back. The room was jammed. If you were as tall as Dick Strout you could probably see over, but the little fellows had a hell of a time because the room was jammed and it got very hot. Roosevelt didn't like air conditioning because it bothered his sinus.

The numbers began to increase with the coming of television. You talk today about the size of the Washington press corps and the number is colossal. But, a large number of those people are technicians who all have to have White House passes—the guy who holds the camera, the guy with the mike, the guys who plug it in, the guys who do lights. You have seen all of this paraphernalia. It's impossible to get them all in one room anywhere.

When Kennedy started using the State Department auditorium television really came into full bloom. But Jim Haggerty started television with Eisenhower in General Pershing's old office, in what originally was the State, War and Navy Building, now the Executive Office Building. Everybody crowded in the small room which wasn't really much bigger than the Oval Office. The seats were really rationed and newspapers and networks were told they couldn't have more than, as I remember, two each. The *New York Times* thought it was entitled to at least three and then the *Washington Post* followed the *New York Times* and so on. But, only when we got to the State Department was there enough space to seat everybody, and then it turned out there was too much space. So, to make it look like Kennedy was attracting a full audience, they put up screens half-way down the auditorium.

QUESTION: Did you experience, as a reporter, any difficulty with the press lords? You talk about the press as having been sympathetic to FDR, but he always said that the newspapers were against him. And they did oppose him often. Did you have any trouble with what you wrote, or did your friends?

MR. ROBERTS: I never did, but I couldn't answer that question fully. In 1932, the press was mixed. Remember, Walter Lippmann said he was a charming governor who was capable of carrying water on both shoulders who thought he ought to be president. Many people misjudged Roosevelt, the same as Walter did. By 1935 he had been so successful in changing, not really the economy, but the mood of the country, that his natural opponents got their breath back and they began to take out after him. The *Washington Post* had been bought at bankruptcy in June of 1933 by Eugene Meyer who had been Herbert Hoover's Chairman of the Federal Reserve Board and had come out of Wall Street. He had very little use, if any, for either Mr. Roosevelt or his New Deal. Mr. Meyer and his wife Agnes went out personally to find a Republican candidate. They had considerable to do with finding a governor in Kansas named Alf Landon, who is still riding horseback at 93, or whatever; and whose daughter is in the Senate. By that time the press barons were on Roosevelt's neck, but he made them look so ridiculous, especially the 1936 *Literary Digest* fiasco, the prediction that Landon would win.

QUESTION: You didn't have trouble getting things printed that you wrote, because of your publisher?

MR. ROBERTS: I never had that kind of trouble. Eugene Meyer was unique in that sense. He let the paper say what it wanted to say. He let the editor say what he wanted to say. He broke with the editor that he first hired, not over the New Deal, but over internationalism and the war and Hitler. Although he was Jewish himself by birth he had been sort of a lapsed Jew, although he refused to go to Germany after Hitler came to power. Nonetheless, he was a strong internationalist and the Washington papers with the largest circulation were strong isolationists papers. The people who had trouble in the sense that you are talking about worked for Hearst, or the *Chicago Tribune,* or the *New York News.* I don't know really where some papers like the *Des Moines Register* were, but most people who disagreed on these points, with those papers, did not work for those papers. They either never tried to work there or if they did, and they fell out, they left. Maybe some were fired. To my knowledge nobody has ever researched that question.

QUESTION: You make the Roosevelt press conference sound like a very useful instrument of social and political policy in the United States. I did not have the good fortune ever to witness one but I have seen some of the more recent ones, and if your description of the Roosevelt press conference is right, things have gone downhill since then. The most recent press conference Reagan gave was typical. It seemed to consist of reasonably useful, intelligent questions that were answered largely by a speech that had been prepared in advance with the big hope that a question would arise in a certain ballpark. The answers thus, obliquely, were related to the question. You feel in watching this that the press are reduced to a rather demeaning role of sitting in a room like school children and shouting for the president's attention, and even when they get it, the president can evade that question very easily.

I wonder if, in your opinion—you have seen a good many press conferences with a good many presidents—you think that the structural changes are of any use in trying to control what a president can get away with in a press conference, or do you think a press conference is ultimately based upon the president's personality and that changes in format won't help? One could, for example, exclude television, allow follow-up questions, ask that questions be submitted in advance, all sorts of possible variations. Do you think it is worthwhile trying to change the format or does the president really have control no matter what?

MR. ROBERTS: I think television has destroyed the press conference as it had destroyed debate in the United States Senate. There's no Webster, Clay, Calhoun kind of debate in the Senate; or even when I came to Washington, Borah, La Follette and Johnson and that crowd that was left over from the isolationist 1920s. There were lines outside the floor of the Senate when people came to listen to them. With the press, I am not sure whether they are schoolboys sitting on benches, but they frequently feel like unpaid actors and sometimes so complain.

Nonetheless, let's look at it from two sides: from the side of the press and the side of the president. From the side of the press, the constant problem, especially at the beginning of any new administration, is to find out, get the measure of the man—so far only a man—and to find out where the locus of power is. It didn't take very long to find out that Ed Meese was a pretty important character in this administration, or that Henry Kissinger was in the Nixon White House, or that Harry Hopkins was in FDR's. You have to find a way of getting behind all those things that are bound in those marvelous collections of presidential papers. A great deal of it was written by bright young men in many cases. Woodrow Wilson, really, I guess, was the last president who wrote his own stuff, so to speak, to any degree. Presidential speechwriting, presidential press relations, press aides are stacked a dozen high. You have to try to get behind that.

One device that always seemed to me to be useful—and I certainly was influenced by the Roosevelt experience—has been the press conference. I've always been an advocate of press conferences at least once a week. It has now just fallen into almost total disuse. I have resisted the idea Scotty Reston is always bringing up. When he had a dull day, he'd write a column about how to reform the press conference. Usually they had to do with suggesting a cabal of senior reporters who would get together like senior diplomats and think up all the wise questions and throw out the trivia. Then we would have a real give and take that would tell us everything. That's baloney. The way you find out something about a president is by surprise. When you listen to Sarah McClenden ask a question of Ronald Reagan it is like two different worlds in collision, and sometimes it doesn't make any sense.

May Craig represented the papers in Portland, Maine for years in Washington, and people wrote about the hats that she wore. But, she had a marvelous way of throwing spit balls at presidents, and sometimes with marvelous results. There is something about being able to ask a question, even though they now have these drill sessions in advance so the press secretary will come out afterwards and say, "You guys were softies. We guessed every question you had." The way you get something, at least it always seemed to me, about the man is from being able to do a face-to-face. And the follow-up question is a very important part of that. They tried to get back to follow-up questions with Carter at one point but television has ruined it—too many ham actors.

That's one of the arguments about getting television into Congress. What I have seen of the televised House proceedings is that it does bring out a certain amount of ham because these segments have been bought by the members of Congress and they send them back to the local TV stations and use it as a campaign thing. The Senate so far has resisted it. I am in favor of letting television in to see what they actually are saying on the Senate floor.

Eisenhower is the best example in a lot of ways beyond what I have said about Roosevelt and the usefulness of the press conference, even though he was the one that introduced television to the press conference. Eisenhower's syntax was notorious, but I never came out of an Eisenhower press conference—and I went to an awful lot of them in the eight years and asked him a lot of questions—where I didn't feel I knew exactly what he said. It was never in the transcript when I wrote it, and I ended up saying that, "The president appeared to mean," or, "It seemed that the president intended to say. . . ." But he had a facility of communication and language just got in his way. You know people like that. Ike was like that. He was a marvelous communicator. When he first set up his press conference, that old fox, John Foster Dulles, arranged to have his the previous day and it gave Eisenhower a way of answering a foreign policy question: "Well, the Secretary answered that yesterday," or, "I reiterate what Secretary Dulles said yesterday." So you had to figure out some way to ask the questions differently. You got into a little bit of matching of wits. You get some sense out of the odd answer as to whom is he depending on in this administration. We haven't got this from Reagan yet. We are beginning to get a little sense of it, but television has basically ruined this kind of press conference. I don't know what the substitute is though.

Now, looking at it from the other side, from the president's side, Theodore Roosevelt was the first modern communicator, in this sense. He was garrulous, he liked to talk to reporters, he had friends among reporters. Like so many presidents, he didn't draw the distinction between the press function and the presidential function. I consider the idea of an adversary relationship to be just as fundamental as the separation of powers. However, it may have created problems. Presidents—and Teddy did this—had favorites, and Herbert Hoover had a medicine ball cabinet and so-called trained seals, including Mark Sullivan who wrote those marvelous books called *Our Times*. Lyndon Johnson felt that if you weren't for him, you were obviously agin' him. Dean Rusk once asked a reporter at a background press conference: "Whose side are you on in Vietnam?" He didn't like some questions about Vietnam. The irony of that was he asked that question of the most pro-administration reporter in the room who was John Scali, then of the AP, now ABC. This is the problem that presidents have. They want you to be part of them, part of their team. It's a problem, it's a terrible problem to resist. Walter Lippmann said that reporters should not get too close to presidents, and in the end he was suckered himself by Lyndon, to his great regret.

Press conferences are an immense value to presidents. Harding started out to do this because he was the one president who had been a publisher, of a small paper in Marion, Ohio. He made a perfect mess of it. He answered some question on the Washington Naval Conference that showed he did not know what he was talking about. And he said: "Boys, you gotta' protect me." That sort of thing. "Besides, it's time for golf." And he had his knickers on. Coolidge was just, he was insolent in a lot of ways. Coolidge actually told reporters not only could they not quote him without his permission, but they could not say, without his permission, that he had refused to answer a question. He created something called "the White House spokesman," who was himself.

Hoover abolished that and he started out at the beginning with a very amicable relationship with the press. After all, he came in with the peak of seeming prosperity. He had been secretary of Commerce, he was well known, he was known in Washington by the press as a highly competent administrator with an engineering background. Then, when the economy began to turn sour, he withdrew more and more. He demanded written questions in advance. The questions that he didn't like were either not handed to him or he threw them in the wastebasket. After the fashion of people in that situation, it just disintegrated. In the end there was no press conference. I think the record shows that between December

1933, that is the month after Roosevelt's election, until the 4th of March, his inauguration—not January 20th—that first time, Hoover saw no press at all. And the country was on the brink of ruin. The banks were closed at the end, and so on. I mean there was absolutely nothing. It was a disastrous relationship.

Roosevelt was, intuitively, an outgoing guy, despite all of his caution and reserve and the things that make him still such a puzzle to historians. After all, he was the first president to fly to a convention that nominated him. He flew to the convention in Chicago, an unheard of thing. Presidents used to wait for some committee to come and tell them what they already knew, that they had been nominated, the McKinley front porch campaign. Roosevelt changed all that. The Depression, of course, made it possible for this. It demanded this, and the response to his change was that people believed the only thing we had to fear was fear itself, that this guy was going to change it, and spirits changed. You can go back and look at the economic record and say the New Deal was a failure in economic terms, but that wasn't the total measure of it. Roosevelt saw that he could command the press conference, and he laid out the ground rules. The press was like a bunch of puppies who hadn't been near a bowl of milk in twenty years. That's why they applauded.

Then he got arrogant about it. The arrogance of power. He was not immune to it. And this business about go stand in the corner started out as a semi-joke, but disintegrated to mean things like the iron cross business. Then he started having less press conferences and there were not very many in the final years. Of course, whether the war was a reasonable reason or not, we would have been better off if there had been more exposure.

But, subsequent presidents have all really based their approach on what Roosevelt discovered and demonstrated—the importance of the press conference. The problem is whether the man has the ability to say, "No comment," or the ability to manage his way around a sticky wicket. Some are better than others, but there's where you find out much about them. I don't know what the answer is, there isn't any answer to the current situation.

It is time for Reagan to have more press conferences. I want to see him face up to more people who are not just syncophants, who are not telling him what they think he wants to hear, which is a terrible problem of the isolation of the White House. But, it is a ragged edge. There is no simple way out of it. This has been sort of a wandering answer to your question.

QUESTION: I have a question about Kennedy rather than Roosevelt but I think it's related to your introductory comments about behind the scenes relations with presidents and the press. What was your role in the suppression of news stories before the

Bay of Pigs invasion, and do you think Kennedy acted legitimately in asking for that news to be suppressed?

MR. ROBERTS: My own role was rather ignominious and it's all in my book. Not since Roosevelt had any president captured the, I guess, imagination of the press as a group as did Jack Kennedy. He was such a charming guy, and a disarming guy. He said the most outrageous things in private to members of the press. Instinctively, you knew you didn't want to hear them because you didn't know exactly what you would do with these things, especially after eight Eisenhower years of a five star general in the White House. Ike considered being a five star general a greater honor than being president and when he retired he wanted to be called General Eisenhower.

Jack Kennedy was a fresh face and a literate man. You must remember that reporters are writers and they love people who can use words, because that's their trade. This is why so many of them liked Adlai Stevenson, although he drove them crazy because he could never get finished with any speech. But he was marvelous. The words sang. Jack Kennedy was the same. Whether Ted Sorenson wrote any given part of them or not is immaterial; he knew how to say it and how to speak it. So, he started with a plus, just as Roosevelt did with that first press conference performance. And the Bay of Pigs was a disaster that he got into. I concluded in my own mind long afterwards that he was too young to be president. If he had been in the Senate another term, then he probably would have been right. That wasn't the way it happened.

The relationship with Cuba to American history is really incredible in so many ways. When Kennedy came in and he found that this CIA program of the Eisenhower years was there waiting. I think he was burdened. I am sure he was burdened by the narrowness of his election which was a shock to him, especially if you remember the night of the election; it started out in the East as though he was going to sweep the country. In fact, Bob Donovan who is a great journalist, pulled one of the great boo-boos of history. He wrote the lead in the *New York Herald Tribune* first edition, something to the effect that: John F. Kennedy is on the way to the greatest sweep since Franklin Roosevelt. It is one of those things that you cringe about afterwards. Jack Kennedy was burdened by the narrowness of this victory and he didn't have the guts to call the damn thing off. He had seniors like Allen Dulles looking over his shoulder saying: "Mr. President, this was all worked out during the Eisenhower years and the agencies and the Joint Chiefs. . .," and all that stuff. He let himself be conned into this.

Some magazine, actually I think it was the *Nation,* by some off chance had a piece from some correspondent who had been in Cen-

tral America and had run across this training ground in Guatemala.
I think that, if I remember correctly, has all been pretty well
documented by Tad Szulc and others, but nobody paid any attention to that. One of the problems of news is that if it doesn't get
Washingtonized somehow or other, it doesn't really get
disseminated everywhere. When the *New York Times* got around to
it they had a number of people who began to pick up the vibes of
this thing. Tad Szulc and some others were down in Florida and
Guatemala and they got this story together. Tad had this long
famous story that got semi-censored. I think it was basically about
what was going on in Guatemala and about the CIA connection.
The *Times* was going to lead the paper with it, and New York asked
Scotty, who was then the bureau chief, "What about this?" and
did he want to double check it. It ended up with Scotty recommend-
ing that they play it down, and they took out some paragraphs and
put it down by the middle of the fold under a one column head, I
think. But, it was a shattering story with that. It was not totally
censored, it was semi-censored, I guess you would say, on the urg-
ing of the administration through Scotty to New York.

By chance the next day I had an appointment to see Kennedy and
this Cuban thing had been sort of at the back of our heads at the
Post but we hadn't focused on it. We didn't have anybody in
Florida but I had read this Tad Szulc story that morning, so I immediately asked Kennedy about it. And he said, "I don't want to
talk about Cuba." I could see he was in a very negative mood about
it, so I tried to work around to it. We talked about Berlin, and
domestic politics, and I don't know what else. I came back to Cuba
a couple of times and finally he said, "Goddamnit," and picked up
the telephone and called the CIA. He got Dick Bissell who was running this Bay of Pigs thing. I heard one-half of this conversation,
during part of which he said, "Do you think I ought to talk to
Reston, to Scotty?" And so on. Then he turned to me and said,
"There are no Americans going to be in anything, we are not going
to get into Cuba." You remember he had drawn a public line between things that were going on among Cubans, Cuban patriots so-
called, and what the United States was doing. In the next day or
two after this broke, after the debacle started, I began to realize
that I had had a smell of this and I didn't write a damn thing about
it, you know, and I kicked myself from here to hell about it. I
didn't know what to do with it.

I did go back, I think, and talk to our editors about it and I guess
the truth of the matter is that we were in such an anti-Castro frame
of mind, we got suckered into being, not apologists but semi-
apologists for the administration, and not doing what we should
have done. The *New York Times,* by censoring the story, was not
as bad because at least they had something. Kennedy told Turner
Catledge, the managing editor of the *New York Times* afterwards,
as you well know, "If you had printed that story," meaning if they

would have given it more display because it actually was printed, "I wouldn't have gotten into this mess." Well, that was a semi-alibi. The press was not good. The wire associations were not good. Part of that I think, was attributable to the Kennedy charisma and charm and the voodo he had on the press, too much of it, as an institution.

Of course the debacle gave everybody such a jolt we all began to sort of reappraise our positions, and I suppose in a way there was more negative stuff written as a retribution of our mistakes or something. That has never been researched to my knowledge, either. There have been a lot of things written in criticism. It was not our finest hour.

QUESTIONS: Wasn't the dilemma a good bit greater than that though? I mean, the business of facts and so forth is one thing, but if the press was going to crack that story at that particular time wouldn't the press have had to be ready to be held in the public eye as being at least partially responsible for removing the element of surprise and defeating the operation?

MR. ROBERTS: Russ Wiggins who was the editor of the paper then, and ran the paper, was a tough anti-Castro guy. He wrote tough anti-Castro editorials and I guess we were permeated by this. It rubbed off on us. I don't think we looked at it as a dilemma. Maybe we should have. We looked at it as though it would be a great thing if the government would knock this guy off.

QUESTION: You would have been a hero, of course, if the Bay of Pigs had succeeded.

MR. ROBERTS: No, Kennedy would have been a hero.

QUESTION: Well, you would have been, too, for holding tight. But are you not really constantly faced with the problem of news vs. national interest that the war brought out very well in terms of responsibility? To what extent is that still something that you constantly have to grapple with?

MR. ROBERTS: World War II was easy because we knew we were on the right side and the other guys were the black hat enemy. But things are not always simple. They got very messy in Vietnam. The only story about which that I remember thinking, "Should this story be printed in the national interest?" had to do with the U-2. Somehow or other before Francis Gary Powers was shot down, after we had started flying over the Soviet Union, the European end of it, but before they started these long flights south to north that Powers was on, I heard from some guy who shouldn't have told me that we're overflying the Soviet Union, taking photographs, and we're really learning something. You remember that we were in missile gaps and all that kind of stuff. I remember coming back to the office with this startling piece of information and talking to the editors. What do you do with this piece? Print this kind of a story? If you print it on the front page of the *Washington Post,* Khrushchev would go through the roof, and the *Washington Post* will be accused of disarming the United States. Well, these are very sticky questions. We had absolutely no question in our mind. The answer was: no, we don't print it. And we didn't. Now, should we have printed it? I still think it is a hard call.

Now, the Pentagon Papers are very different. I was a defendant in that case by chance because I wrote the first story that the *Post* printed after we suffered from the *New York Times* for several days. In that case, we ended up in a courtroom in Washington, where the judge threw everybody out of the courtroom except the lawyers and the defendants. This was so that we could hear the government present its case, certain parts of its case, some of which was later done in camera. We even heard that further publication was a threat to the lives of American soldiers and to the diplomacy of the country. The adjectives rolled a mile high. It was absolute crap. We ended up by going out between sessions and getting a number of books off shelves and clippings out of newspapers and rushing back in to show the judge that a great deal of this had already been in the public print. The government had just not collected it together. The Solicitor General of the United States, a former Dean of the Harvard Law School, if I remember correctly, got so exasperated with the Pentagon and the State Department, which kept saying, "You can't let them print anything," that he finally said something to the effect: "Give me four examples of the damage it will do and let it boil down to something I can present to the Court." Well, we went through this exercise of very frightening stuff. I felt I was being charged with treason by the time I got through. It was absolutely absurd, the kind of things the government said. The National Security Agency came in, sent some Admiral in, talking about codes and how we were going to destroy the security of the United States. At least one thing Daniel Ellsberg had done, he had put a piece of paper over the top of the coding stuff on these various sheets that he was running through the mill before he started giving them out. Besides, those things change. We had to bring in a code expert to show that this was an absurdity that he was talking about. This was the kind of thing that the government will do to you, if you give them half a chance, to protect what they say is their secret.

By the time it got up to the Supreme Court and the *Times* and the *Post* cases were joined, the thing had shaken down to the point where the Justices wanted to know what damage had been caused and what damage might be caused and how did the government know this damage would be caused. Really, we got out of it by a fluke. The Court really said that you should not have proceeded with an injunction to prevent the publication. You should have come into Court after they had published something, not in prior restraint. But they left a sloppy record. The Court was far from one mind. It opened the press up to a lot of subsequent problems and the Court is still doing this. The Court's problem with the press is partly the press's problem too.

To talk about this for a moment more, part of it is Watergate and part of it is to perceive the arrogance of the press, including the *Washington Post*. The *Post* got sued yesterday by Jimmy Carter. He announced they are going to sue the paper on what is a really pretty good case in the sense of public policy. I don't know whether it is a legal case or not, but there are a lot of these hazy issues that keep arising. My feeling has always been that it is a foolish thing to try to draw sharp legal lines as to what the press should or shouldn't do. Both the press and the public are better off if a gray area is allowed. And when you have a sharp case you can make a distinction on that case. I think someone said bad cases make bad law and this is certainly true. In the *Pentagon Papers* case it wasn't a good case.

NARRATOR: I think the University president to whom the University will shortly pay final tribute would have been thrilled at this discussion. Governor Colgate Darden told us on numerous occasions that he was delighted we were having such things as Miller Center Forums, and I think he would have been particularly happy today. Maybe that's the best way to say thank you, as some of us leave for a memorial service for a great political and educational leader.

A CONCLUDING NOTE

The successes and failures of recent presidents demonstrate the urgent need for a deeper understanding of the fundamentals of the American presidency. One route to understanding the most powerful executive office in the world is clearly through research and writing. The Miller Center in terms of its allocation of resources has overwhelmingly given highest priority to this approach. The centerpiece of its program is scholarly research.

At the same time, other routes to knowledge need not be neglected. One such approach is an examination of particular presidencies through discussions with leaders who were close to the center of activities. In this regard, the Miller Center is turning to those who are the survivors of certain landmark administrations.

We were fortunate in bringing four such extraordinary observers as Thomas G. Corcoran, James Rowe, Franklin D. Roosevelt, Jr. and Chalmers Roberts to this common enterprise. As fate would have it, one of the four is no longer with us, a possibility that spurs us on in seeking portraits of other presidents.